MELBA'S AMERICAN COMFORT

MELBA'S AMERICAN COMFORT

100 Recipes from My Heart to Your Kitchen

MELBA WILSON
PHOTOGRAPHY BY MELISSA HOM

ATRIA BOOKS

New York London Toronto Sydney New Delhi

ATRIA BOOKS

An Imprint of Simon & Schuster, Inc.
1230 Avenue of the Americas
New York, NY 10020

First Atria Books hardcover edition April 2016

ATRIA BOOKS and colophon are trademarks of Simon & Schuster, Inc.

For information about special discounts for bulk purchases, please contact Simon & Schuster Special Sales at 1-866-506-1949 or business@simonandschuster.com.

The Simon & Schuster Speakers Bureau can bring authors to your live event. For more information or to book an event contact the Simon & Schuster Speakers Bureau at 1-866-248-3049 or visit our website at www.simonspeakers.com.

Interior design by Jason Snyder
Photography by Melissa Hom

Manufactured in China

10 9 8 7 6 5 4 3 2 1

Library of Congress Cataloging-in-Publication Data has been applied for.

ISBN 978-1-4767-9528-7
ISBN 978-1-4767-9531-7 (ebook)

My Dear Salif, like this book, you too are my first, my one, my only. You inspire me to work hard, laugh heartily, and love harder all while savoring life's moments. Thank you for loving me in spite of and regardless. This one, my first, is for you!

Love, Mom

CONTENTS

INTROD

I was born, bred, and buttered in Harlem, and I spent my summer vacations with my grandparents in the Carolinas—a welcome, relaxing getaway from New York City life.

I honed my people and entrepreneurial skills at the Ophelia DeVore School of Charm in midtown Manhattan and working at the world famous Sylvia's Soul Food Restaurant in Harlem before opening my own, but I actually learned to cook in my grandmother's kitchen. Grandma Amelia (or Mea, as we called her) mixed love with every ingredient that went into her down-home country comfort cooking—and she made some of the best food I've ever tasted!

Like most Americans, I'm something of a hybrid—formed both by my family's Southern heritage and by our equally strong connection to the uniquely rich culture, music, and art of Harlem, where I still live today.

My grandma Mea was my favorite girl. She was much more than just a grandmother to me. She was my best friend, my confidante, my advisor, and my rock. She taught me the importance of family, loyalty, honesty, and love. Whenever I talk about good times growing up, she's one of the first people who come to mind. Grandma Mea had nine children, fourteen grandchildren, nineteen great-grandchildren, and a lot of wisdom. I still find myself quoting her favorite "isms," including, "So good it makes me wanna slap my momma," "Don't let the door hit you where the good Lord split you," and "Only a hit dog howls." One

that I, luckily, haven't found to be true (at least for me) is, "Those people from up North, they'll offer you a drink, but don't ask them for no food."

ᵍᵉᵍᵉᵍᵉᵍᵉᵍᵉᵍᵉᵍᵉᵍᵉᵍᵉᵍᵉ

As a young girl, whenever I was in South Carolina, I could usually be found in Mea's kitchen, "noseying up" to see what she was doing and how much of this or that ingredient she was putting in, and marveling at how she always managed to get things right. Back in Harlem, I also spent a lot of time watching my mom, Tina Wilson, cook at our home on 138th Street off Lenox Avenue.

Back then, us kids weren't allowed to cook. Cooking was strictly the job of the woman of the house, the highly prestigious domain of the queen. My mother was definitely the queen of our castle, which meant that I spent my first ten years watching, learning, and taking mental notes.

Although I wasn't allowed to join in, I *was* allowed to lick the cake bowls. And lick them I did! Any time my mother or grandmother baked a cake, they would first make a five-inch sample. I think they did that because they knew their baking was so good that us kids would never have the patience to wait until dinnertime for a slice. The sample sufficed to hold us over while protecting the full-size cake from being eaten and our hands from getting popped for trying to eat it!

I devoured, I soooo devoured, the extra batter left in the bowls and the tasting samples; but I also yearned to bake my own cakes. My first real baking experience came when I was about twelve or thirteen, and, boy, was I excited! My uncle LeRoy Dorsey, who sang in a gospel group called the Sensational Starlights of CT, loooovvvved cake almost as much as I did. But Uncle Roy was diabetic and wasn't supposed to have sweets. So I came up with a spice cake recipe that he could safely enjoy. It had cinnamon, allspice, cloves, and nutmeg for flavor. I also used applesauce for sweetness and to keep it nice and moist. It was the first cake I was ever allowed to bake, and I baked it with pride and joy for Uncle Roy every time the Starlights sang in New York.

Both my parents came from large families. Mom was the youngest of eleven children—six girls and five boys—and grew up in Andrews, South Carolina, wearing hand-me-downs, already handed down five times before they got to her. Her family was poor, but I guess they didn't really know it because they had each other and never went hungry.

We weren't rich either, and we didn't have an excess of material items, but we had a great family. We were rich in spirit, and visited each other every weekend. When you're a kid, that's what truly matters, and I still depend on family as my foundation.

My father's family, from Hemingway, about twenty-five miles north of Andrews, was the opposite of my mom's. He was one of nine kids, his father owned a thriving grocery store and gas station, and my father opened his own business—a barber shop—when he was in his twenties. Theirs was the first household in town to have a television.

I was also blessed to have a stepfather, Louis Wilson, who raised me from the age of two as if I were his own flesh and blood. Some of my fondest memories are of the times I spent baking cakes in my Easy-Bake oven with his nieces, my cousins Tessey and Jen. His parents, Grandma Easter and Grandpa Babe Wilson, were also huge inspirations in my life.

Other than a lot of kids, one thing all three families had in common was that food was king. Every celebration, every special occasion started with a prayer and ended with a home-cooked meal. Preparing and sharing food was one way to spread the love. There was an element of pitching in, but there was also pride and underlying competitiveness. All those home cooks set the bar high. You just wouldn't show up at a church or community function with anything but your Sunday best. When all the food was laid out, the same questions always hovered in the air: Who made the best potato salad? The best macaroni and cheese? Or, more important, the best pie?

Whenever I go back to South Carolina, I always make time to cook a special meal. There's something therapeutic about it for me, particularly when I'm cooking in my grandmother's kitchen and with my aunt Dona. She always teases me: "Okay, so we're going to do a throwdown. You beat Bobby Flay; now can you beat me?"

The funny thing is that, for a long time, Aunt Dona was a really terrible cook and was known for having nothing but bottled water and Pepsi-Cola in her refrigerator. It wasn't until she went back down south to take care of my grandmother after my grandfather died that she actually learned to cook. Now she is one of the finest home cooks I know.

To my mind, cooks like my mom, grandma Mea, and my aunt Dona are true gems, as inspirational as all the dedicated professionals I've worked with. They're doing it for their families, their churches, their synagogues, their communities. They're doing it for love, which, as a kid, I was told to do something that you love (and get paid for too), that way you will never "work" a day in your life!

I have more than a hundred cousins, and several of my family members had country names in addition to their given first names: Cousin William was Pigball; there was Inkspot, and Tootsie; my mom was Sistah, and Aunt Dona was always Duck. To this day some of my cousins still refer to her as Aunt Duck.

When I was a kid, every summer we all gathered down south. My brother and sister went kicking and screaming, but for some of us city kids, it was a wonderful taste of life on a working farm and a great way to connect with our extended families. We spent most of our time outdoors, and it seemed like every day we could go to a different cousin's house. Every house had a vegetable garden and everybody had hogs and chickens—that's how we ate. We would collect the eggs from the barn, get milk from the cows, and pull the tomatoes off the vine. We practiced genuine farm-to-table cooking long before that catchphrase took over the foodie world.

These days, people in Hemingway don't have a lot of farm animals, but some still have thriving gardens, and I still get the same warm feelings of relaxation and comfort when I go there. My grandma Mea passed away in 2010 at the age of one hundred, but her spirit is very much with us. Sometimes when I get caught up in the hustle and bustle, the fast pace, the bright lights of New York City, I know it's time to take a long weekend and head down south. Being close to nature, being in my grandmother's house, and marinating in her memories reenergizes and rejuvenates me to return to my hectic city life—running a busy restaurant, a cafeteria, and a catering operation; raising a teenage son as a divorced mom; staying abreast of everything going on in my community. I am not complaining. I love my life!

It's true that, like so many generations of women, I learned to cook in my mother's and grandmother's kitchens. But my first interests and skills were as a salesperson and entrepreneur, not as a restaurateur or caterer. I attended Ophelia DeVore's School of Charm, which was located in the prestigious Ed Sullivan Theater on the corner of Fifty-Third Street and Broadway in Manhattan, New York. Even as a preteen, I took pride in being able to outsell the adults at Ophelia DeVore's Beauty Bar. Ms. DeVore was one of my first and most influential role models—a determined, elegant, independent black businesswoman.

Back in the late 1940s, Ms. DeVore, who was fair-skinned enough to pass for white, had been taking lessons at the Vogue School of Modeling. She'd never even considered that the people at the school didn't know she was black until, one day, a brown-skinned girl walked in and was immediately told that they didn't admit colored people. That incident was the catalyst that inspired Ms. DeVore to start the first black modeling agency. She went on to launch the career of Helen Williams, the first African American model, as well as those of Diahann Carroll, Cicely Tyson, and many others. I did some modeling myself when I was young and could certainly identify with that brown-skinned girl who got turned away.

I first met Ms. DeVore when I was about ten years old, and, by thirteen, I was taking one of her classes every Saturday. I would arrive early to help out in the office, stuffing envelopes, and, after class, I would sell cosmetics at the beauty bar. The goal at the back of my mind each week was to sell more makeup than any of the adults. And that's what I did!

I discovered if I truly believed in what I was selling—whether it was eyeliner and blush or fried chicken and greens—I felt really great about sharing it with others. It made *me* happy to see how happy a product could make a customer, and I guess my excitement was contagious.

After college, a partner and I started a service called Rent-A-Chauffeur, which provided drivers for people who owned their own cars but didn't want to drive themselves. It was a lot less expensive than renting a chauffeur-driven limo, and the business did very well, but after two and a half years I no longer found it satisfying. I was chained to a desk with a phone attached to my ear, talking to clients, taking their credit card information, and to drivers, scheduling pickups.

Around that time, in 1987, Sylvia Woods asked me to organize her restaurant's twenty-fifth-anniversary celebration. I put together a three-day event, including a community gathering, a gospel breakfast, and a black-tie gala for more than nine hundred people. It was a huge success, and shortly thereafter she offered me a full-time job in the restaurant. I started as a cashier and loved it; graduated to become a hostess and loved that; then assisted with catering, and I loved that, too.

From the moment I started at Sylvia's, I knew this was what I wanted to do. I just fell in love with the restaurant business. It didn't feel like work. People would often come up and ask if I were Sylvia, and at first I'd get annoyed. I was in my twenties at the time and the restaurant was more than twenty-five years old. How could I possibly be Sylvia? Eventually, though, it dawned on me that what they were saying was that my work ethic, attitude, and enthusiasm showed I wasn't just in it for the paycheck, and I started to take it as a compliment. I worked at Sylvia's for eleven years and that is where I got my "Ph.D." in the restaurant business.

I adored Sylvia. They say that imitation is the sincerest form of flattery, and I knew I could imitate but never duplicate her. She was the queen. She was also my business role model. Both she and Ophelia DeVore instilled in me the conviction that if I wrote down my dreams, believed in my dreams, and worked hard, I would surely achieve them. Even to this day I can hear Sylvia saying, "You can do this, Champ!"

In addition to teaching me indispensable skills, working my way up at Sylvia's provided me with some great business connections. In 1992 I was taken under the wing of one of New York's most prominent restaurateurs, Drew Nieporent, who offered me some fantastic opportunities. Somehow they didn't come together, but that was okay. I was learning more and more about the business, and all along I knew that God had a plan for me.

Among the many people I met through Drew was Josefina Howard of the Rosa Mexicano restaurant empire, and around 1996 I went to work for her. I started in the back of the house (aka the kitchen), learning every ingredient in every dish, and then moved to the front. At Rosa Mexicano, I perfected the art of taking care of my clientele. I also saw firsthand that presenting food with passion, conviction, and love is a winning formula. Miss Howard, as we called her, was wonderful; I just loved her. Who didn't? She was another great, strong, female role model and professional mentor.

Born in Cuba, she was raised in Spain and spent much of her young adult life in Mexico. At her restaurant, she served Mexican food with a modern twist and built a tremendously loyal following with a big-city A-list clientele. Somewhere deep inside, the idea was percolating that I could do the same with my own traditional style of cooking.

Meanwhile, I got married and set up my own home. Finally, I had a chance to turn *my* own kitchen into a warm, welcoming place for family and friends, just as my grandmother had done with hers. I knew how happy it made her to cook for the people she loved . . . and I realized that I could do the same. To this day, I never cook "just enough" for whoever is in the house. I always cook for "just in case". . . as in, just in case a friend drops by, just in case the neighbor smells the food, just in case a cousin happens to be in town. Worst-case scenario, leftovers!

Cooking is my therapy. When I'm stressed, cooking takes me to a wonderful faraway place. In fact, very often I've already tasted my way through an entire meal by the time dinner is served.

After I married in 1999, I continued working at Rosa Mexicano until a month before my son, Salif, was born. At that point I knew it was time for me to leave so that I could devote myself to spending quality time with him. But I didn't lose touch with the restaurant business entirely. Having instituted and organized a highly successful gospel brunch at Sylvia's, I was contacted by Chef Michael Lomonaco and his colleagues at Windows on the World to do the same for their restaurant. I did it, and within six months, their Sunday revenues increased by 65 percent. Unfortunately, that all ended tragically on 9/11. Never forget . . .

By 2004, Salif wasn't a baby anymore—he was in school and he could talk to me to let me know if anything went wrong. Also, around that time, my marriage was breaking up. I was on an airplane one day and, for some reason, that same old announcement I'd heard flight attendants make hundreds of times—"In case of an emergency, put on your own mask first and then take care of others"—took on a completely different meaning. It hit me that, as a caregiver, taking care of others wasn't quite enough. I had to look in the mirror and start taking care of me. It was time to open my own restaurant.

In 2005, sadly, Josefina Howard died, but her business partners, Doug Griebel and Dan Hickey, have continued to build on Rosa Mexicano's success. Of course, I knew them both well and we had kept in touch after I left the restaurant. In 2005, they opened a big new branch on East Eighteenth Street in the space that had been occupied by another well-known restaurant, America. They were redecorating, and since they knew I was also in the process of opening Melba's, they asked me to come and look at the furniture, equipment, and cutlery they weren't going to be keeping to see if there was anything I could use. My assumption was that they would charge me for whatever I took; but, in fact, they gave it all to me for FREE. Doug and Dan's generosity saved me many thousands of dollars and, to this day, much of the silverware, bathroom sinks, as well as the bar stools at Melba's, come from America.

Although I entered the food-service business through the back door of customer service and marketing, I never forgot my roots in Grandma Mea's kitchen. From the moment I opened the doors at Melba's in July 2005, the "default setting" has been the classic recipes of my Carolina heritage with a dash of extra spice, a little urban edge, a taste of the melting pot, and a few "dee-lish" twists. My cooking philosophy starts with the freshest local ingredients, because that's what my family has used for so long.

Another major theme in my restaurant and catering business is family-style service, which follows in the tradition of church and backyard cookouts, where everybody brings something and it's a potluck feast.

Melba's Five Lessons for Life In and Out of the Kitchen

I'm still working on these, so let's put them in the pot and stir it up together.

1. Remember to say "I appreciate you." I learned this lesson working in a restaurant kitchen, where we almost never got to hear that what we were doing was appreciated by the people dining in the front of the house. Everyone appreciates knowing they are appreciated.

2. Say something nice to someone you don't know. You never know how that might change their day.

3. Surprise someone with something unexpected that makes them smile.

4. Never say "I can't." All that does is limit what's possible for you. When you actually accomplish what you thought you couldn't, the feeling is euphoric.

5. We cooks tend to be caregivers. We get joy from taking care of others, but we need to let others feel that joy too by allowing them to take care of us.

—Love you, M

Like the dishes I serve at Melba's, many of the recipes in this book, the staples —collard greens, fried chicken, and sweet potato pie—have been passed down from one generation to the next, with each of us adding a little something to make it our own, similar to a new arrangement of a standard song. As a result, recipes such as spring rolls, chipotle mayo dipping sauce, and wine-braised short ribs, to name a few, add Asian, Latin, and sophisticated urban or continental influences to their Southern roots.

Our fried chicken and waffles is a perfect example of this. Any self-respecting home cook knows how to make a mean fried chicken; I learned it from my mother and grandmother. But *fried chicken and waffles* is a Harlem creation through and through. I developed the eggnog waffles on my own, out of necessity, a willingness to experiment, and an openness to serendipity. A little improvisation and adaptation can come in handy, and at Melba's,

Fried Chicken and Eggnog Waffles—my version of the Harlem classic—is now a signature dish.

Over the years, Harlem has become an international tourist destination and brand—for good reason. It's the cultural and artistic heart of black America, where soul music and soul food found their launching pads. Nobody who has performed the music or cooked the food has ever forgotten their roots in Harlem *or* their deep connections to the South . . . and neither have I.

My intimate corner spot at 114th Street and Frederick Douglass Boulevard is my flagship, but the heart and soul of my cooking is still rooted in my grandmother's kitchen and the home kitchens of all of us who cook in our ancestors' footsteps. With this book, I aim to share that spirit and those recipes so you can bring them into your kitchen for your own family to enjoy as mine has for generations.

As far as comfort-cooking goes, the first thing I say is: "If I can do it, you can, too!" That's because I *am* the girl next door. These recipes are simple, foolproof, true to their down-home spirit, and dedicated to at-home success. There are no mysterious secrets; all it takes is love and desire, along with a few time-tested ingredients and techniques. So, dig in, have fun, and enjoy all the delicious food and great times my family has enjoyed for years—and still does.

Hugs and Sweet Potato Pie Kisses,
Melba Wilson

AUTHOR'S NOTE

At the top of certain recipes throughout this book, you will find an icon ☺☺, indicating that they are my go-to choices when I'm cooking for a crowd. They may be easily doubled, made in advance and served at room temperature or reheated, or just one-pot meals.

Use these as a guide, but if you want to experiment with others, I urge you to do that, too.

MELBA'S AMERICAN COMFORT

1

BREAKFAST & BRUNCH

MELBA'S EGGNOG WAFFLES

One morning when my son, Salif, was about five years old, he said he wanted waffles for breakfast, but when I checked the fridge, I realized there was no milk. All I had was eggnog and orange juice. Clearly there wasn't any choice, so I made them with eggnog.

They came out great, and my son went to school happy.

When I opened my restaurant a few months later, I put them on the menu alongside the fried chicken (see recipe on page 132). A few years later, when I went up against Bobby Flay on the Food Network program *Throwdown with Bobby Flay*, my version stole the show—much to Bobby's surprise.

Salif is now in high school, and he never ceases to remind me when he wants to get his way with something that if it weren't for him I'd never have made those award-winning eggnog waffles.

For me, the dish represents tradition, serendipity, resourcefulness, and family cooking at its best. It's a fun, delicious tweak on a soul food classic—and that's exactly what I like to do: honor our roots while also updating and elevating the genre.

You can have your waffles for breakfast, lunch, or dinner, with fried chicken or on their own, topped with Strawberry Butter (page 6), peaches, blueberries, maple syrup, or anything else that sounds good to you.

MAKES 4 WAFFLES

2 cups all-purpose flour, sifted

2 teaspoons baking powder

Pinch of ground cinnamon

Pinch of ground nutmeg

1½ to 2 cups eggnog,* homemade (recipe follows) or store-bought

2 large eggs, separated

4 tablespoons (½ stick) unsalted butter, melted

Nonstick cooking spray, for the waffle iron
Strawberry Butter (recipe follows), optional

. . . .

Start with 1½ cups before deciding whether your batter needs more. As the saying goes, you can always add more, but you can never take away. What I normally do—and what I suggest that you do—is make one as a sample and check to see if it's puffy enough and moist enough on the inside. Based on that, you can decide whether or not to add more.

1. In a large bowl, combine the flour, baking powder, cinnamon, and nutmeg. In another bowl, whisk together the eggnog, egg yolks, and melted butter. Stir the wet ingredients into the dry ingredients just until combined. The batter shouldn't be lumpy, but don't overmix it.

2. In a clean bowl, whisk the egg whites until almost stiff, and fold them into the batter.

3. Heat a waffle iron and spray it with nonstick cooking spray. Ladle one quarter cup of the batter into the middle of the hot iron and close the lid. Cook for 3 to 4 minutes, until cooked through and golden brown. Repeat with the remaining batter, respraying the waffle iron before each addition.

4. Serve with the strawberry butter, if desired.

EGGNOG

This will keep tightly covered in the refrigerator for up to one week.

MAKES 6 TO 8 CUPS

1½ cups whole milk
½ cup heavy cream
1 tablespoon pure vanilla extract
½ teaspoon ground cinnamon
Pinch of ground nutmeg
4 large eggs, separated, plus 2 yolks
¾ cup sugar
2 ounces rum or bourbon (optional), or to taste

1. Combine the milk and cream in a saucepot over medium-low heat and bring to a slow boil. Whisk in the vanilla, cinnamon, and nutmeg. Place the 6 egg yolks in a large heat-proof mixing bowl. Slowly ladle half the milk and cream mixture into the yolks, whisking vigorously. Pour the mixture back into the pot with the rest of the milk and cream, raise the heat to high, and continue whisking until the mixture thickens to the consistency of a loose pudding. Transfer the mixture back to the bowl, cover with plastic wrap, and refrigerate to chill.

2. While the yolk mixture is chilling, place the 4 egg whites in the bowl of an electric mixer. Using a whisk attachment, mix on high until they begin to thicken. Continue beating as you gradually add the sugar; the whites will continue to stiffen. Remove the yolk mixture from the fridge, hand whisk in the beaten whites, stir in the rum or bourbon if you like, and serve.

STRAWBERRY BUTTER

 1 cup (2 sticks) unsalted butter, slightly softened
 4 ounces strawberries, hulled and sliced (about ½ cup)
 A few drops of grenadine syrup

1. Put the butter in a food processor fitted with a metal blade and blend until smooth. Add the strawberries and grenadine and pulse until there are just a few small pieces of berry visible.

2. Serve at once with your waffles or refrigerate until needed.

SWEET POTATO WAFFLES

When I think of sweet potatoes, so many sweet, wonderful memories come to mind. Sweet potatoes are very comforting. Whether they're baked, candied, in the sweet potato pancakes (see variation on next page), or in these waffles, they always remind me of my grandmother's hugs. I guess that's why I just love sweet potatoes.

MAKES 3 TO 4 WAFFLES

2 medium sweet potatoes

1½ cups whole wheat flour

¼ cup sugar

1 tablespoon baking powder

½ teaspoon kosher salt

½ teaspoon ground cinnamon

Pinch of ground nutmeg

1 cup half-and-half*

4 tablespoons (½ stick) unsalted butter, melted

3 large eggs, separated, at room temperature

Nonstick cooking spray or vegetable oil or butter, for the waffle iron

. . . .

My son likes his sweet potato waffles made with vanilla coconut milk. Try it and see if you like it.

1. Drop the sweet potatoes, in their skins, into a pot of boiling water and cook until fork-tender, about 25 minutes. When cool enough to handle, peel off the skin (it will come off easily) and mash the potatoes. Measure and set aside ½ cup. (If there's any left over, enjoy it while you finish cooking.)

2. Preheat the waffle iron.

3. In a large bowl, whisk together the flour, sugar, baking powder, salt, cinnamon, and nutmeg until well combined.

4. In another bowl, whisk together the half-and-half, mashed potatoes, melted butter, and the egg yolks.

5. In a small bowl, with an electric hand mixer, whisk the egg whites on high speed until they form stiff peaks, about 2 minutes. Set aside.

6. Make a well in the center of the dry ingredients and pour in the wet ingredients. Whisk together, starting slowly, until well combined but not overmixed.

7. Gently fold in the beaten egg whites, making sure not to deflate them.

8. Spray the waffle iron with nonstick cooking spray or brush it with a bit of vegetable oil or butter and pour in enough of the batter to fill it halfway. The waffles will rise as they cook, and the amount of batter will vary from one waffle iron to another. Close the lid and cook for 3 to 4 minutes, until cooked through and golden brown. Repeat with the remaining batter, respraying the waffle iron before each addition.

9. Serve with butter, maple syrup, whipped cream, fresh fruit, ice cream, or with chicken instead of the Eggnog Waffles. Any way you eat them, they're sweet potato good!

Variation: To make sweet potato pancakes use 1½ cups of half-and-half, and cook as you would the buttermilk pancakes on page 11.

Cleaning Your Waffle Iron

There are many different kinds of waffle irons and many different suggestions for how to clean them. Some say to never touch it until it's completely cooled, but one of my favorite suggestions (because it seems the easiest) is to UNPLUG IT (very important) and, while it's still hot, place a wet (but not dripping) paper towel on the surface, close the lid, and let it steam itself clean for a few minutes. Then, while it's still warm, wipe away any lingering crumbs.

If you still have the manufacturer's instruction booklet that came with the iron, I'd recommend that you follow the directions in that!

SALIF'S SATURDAY MORNING BUTTERMILK PANCAKES

On Saturday mornings when Salif wakes up and asks for pancakes, I remind him of the rule: If that's what he wants, he has to help. It's always fun because it's something we get to do together. He likes to prepare the dry ingredients. I mix the wet ingredients. Then he makes the well in the center of the dry ingredients and combines the two. The only thing I won't let him do is the actual cooking, because he doesn't have the patience to wait until bubbles form to flip the pancakes. As soon as he sees a single bubble, he's got the spatula in his hand. Actually, I confess that, to speed up the process, I sometimes cover the pan to cook the first side. It also makes the pancakes really fluffy. You can't do this if you're using a griddle, however, and you must never cover the pan when cooking the second side or the pancakes will come out wet.

MAKES 8 PANCAKES

2 cups all-purpose flour

2 teaspoons baking powder

1 teaspoon baking soda

¼ cup sugar

1 tablespoon ground cinnamon

1½ cups buttermilk

½ vanilla bean, seeds scraped

4 tablespoons (½ stick) unsalted butter, melted, plus additional for the pan

2 eggs, lightly beaten

1. Sift the flour twice into a medium mixing bowl and stir in the baking powder, baking soda, sugar, and cinnamon. In a separate bowl, combine the buttermilk, vanilla bean seeds, and 4 tablespoons of melted butter. Mix well. Then gently fold in the eggs. Do not overmix. Make a well in the center of the dry ingredients and add the wet. Stir slowly to combine the two. Let the batter sit for 10 to 15 minutes.

2. Brush a griddle or a heavy-bottomed pan with melted butter and set over medium heat. When the pan is hot, pour in ¼ cup of the batter and cook until the top is filled with bubbles. Flip and cook for an additional 3 to 4 minutes on the other side until golden brown.

3. Serve with fresh fruit, maple syrup, jam, bacon, or all of the above. C'mon—it's Saturday!

YUMMY BACON *and* CHEESE SCONES

My love for scones came about when I started spending time in London. On dreary mornings in Hampstead, I would often treat myself to a wonderful cup of tea and a yummy, delish scone. When I got back to the States, I began making scones and incorporating favorites like bacon and cheese, sometimes separate and in this case together, into my version of a scone. Enjoy, mate!

MAKES 8 FRITTERS

½ pound applewood-smoked bacon

2 cups pastry flour

1 tablespoon baking powder

1 teaspoon salt

2 teaspoons sugar

½ cup unsalted butter, cold, cut into chunks

½ cup Asiago cheese, grated

½ cup cheddar cheese, diced

¾ cup heavy cream

1 large egg

¼ cup heavy cream (for brushing and just in case)

1. Preheat the oven to 400 degrees and line your baking sheet with parchment paper.

2. In a frying pan, fry the bacon over medium heat until it is a bit crispy, 4 to 5 minutes. Wrap it in a paper towel to drain the excess oil and then transfer the bacon to your cutting board and finely chop or crumble.

3. In a large mixing bowl, whisk together the flour, baking powder, salt, and sugar. Add the butter and work it into the flour until the mixture looks coarse and crumbly.

4. Add the cheese and bacon and mix until evenly distributed throughout.

5. In a small bowl, whisk together the egg and ¾ cup heavy cream until blended. Combine with the dough and stir until it comes together. If necessary, add additional cream.

6. Transfer the dough onto a well-floured work surface. Bring the dough together into a ball. Using a floured rolling pin, roll out the dough to ½ inch thick. Using a 1½-inch biscuit cutter, cut out as many scones as possible. Take the scraps of dough, roll out, and cut additional scones.

7. Space the scones evenly on your baking sheet and brush with a tad bit of cream. Bake until the scones are golden brown, 15 to 20 minutes. Remove from the oven and let cool slightly before serving.

JOHNNYCAKES

Johnnycakes are basically cornmeal flatbreads, which are said to have originated in New England, where early settlers learned to make them from the local Native Americans. They are, in effect, the New England equivalent of a corn tortilla. Where the name comes from is more or less lost in the sands of time. In fact, they are known by various names—sometimes journey cakes, and, in the South, hoecakes. But a johnnycake by any name will still taste great. Serve them for breakfast instead of pancakes, or with eggs instead of toast.

MAKES 4 TO 6 SILVER-DOLLAR-SIZE CAKES

1 cup yellow self-rising cornmeal*

¾ teaspoon salt

1 teaspoon sugar

1 cup cold water

½ cup whole milk

Bacon drippings or butter, to grease the pan

. . . .

*Can't find self-rising flour or cornmeal? Make your own!
1 cup all purpose flour OR cornmeal, 1½ teaspoons baking powder,
and ¼ teaspoon salt*

1. In a medium, heat-proof bowl, combine the cornmeal, salt, and sugar. Bring the water to a rapid boil in a medium saucepan over high heat. Whisking constantly, slowly pour the boiling water into the cornmeal mixture. Then whisk in the milk. The mixture will be fairly thick and not runny.

2. Generously grease a large frying pan (preferably cast iron) with bacon drippings, if you have them, or butter. When the pan is hot, pour in a tablespoon of the batter, flatten it with a spoon, and cook as you would a pancake. Cook in batches if necessary, adding more drippings or butter as needed.

EGGY FRENCH TOAST

like my French toast very "eggy." If you don't, use three or four eggs instead of five. My favorite breads for this are challah or brioche. Thin-cut breads need not apply—they will collapse under the weight of the other ingredients.

MAKES 6 SERVINGS

2 cups half-and-half

⅓ cup honey, microwaved for 10 to 20 seconds

3 tablespoons unsalted butter, melted, plus 1 teaspoon softened unsalted butter

½ teaspoon pure vanilla extract

½ teaspoon ground cinnamon

¼ teaspoon ground nutmeg

Pinch of salt

5 large eggs, lightly beaten

12 (1-inch-thick) slices of challah or brioche bread

1. In a bowl, combine the half-and-half, microwaved honey, melted butter, vanilla, cinnamon, nutmeg, and salt. Mix in the beaten eggs.

2. Set a 10-inch skillet over low to medium heat and brush the pan with a bit of the softened butter. In batches, add the bread to the batter and let it soak for a couple of seconds on both sides. Transfer the soaked bread to the skillet and cook for 3 to 4 minutes, until brown on the bottom, then flip it over and cook for 2 minutes on the other side. Repeat with the remaining bread, adding a bit more of the softened butter to the pan as you go.

3. Serve with powdered sugar, maple syrup, your favorite fruit, whipped cream, or any of the above.

COLLARD GREENS OMELET

Make this for yourself with leftover collards or, if you have enough, make omelets for your entire family. Don't love collards? Try using the Sautéed Kale and Mushrooms on page 176.

MAKES 1 SERVING

¼ cup Country Collard Greens (page 172)
1 teaspoon potlikker (see page 173)*
3 large eggs
Salt and freshly ground black pepper
1 teaspoon unsalted butter

. . . .

*If you don't have any potlikker, use 1 teaspoon of either chicken broth or water.

1. Heat the potlikker in a small saucepan over medium-high heat. When hot, add the collards and stir to reheat. Remove the pan from the heat and set aside.

2. Lightly beat the eggs with salt and pepper to taste.

3. Heat an 8-inch nonstick sauté or omelet pan over medium heat for 3 minutes, until it is really hot. Add the butter, spreading it around the pan. When the butter begins to bubble, pour the eggs into the middle of the pan and tilt the pan so that the eggs cover the bottom. As they begin to cook, tilt the pan so that the uncooked eggs in the middle flow to the edges. When the eggs are still a bit runny, place the collards in the middle and, using a silicone or rubber spatula, fold the omelet in half or fold the two edges into the middle to make a trifold. Gently slide the omelet out of the pan and onto a plate. You can use your spatula to help with this.

2
COMFORTIZERS

EAST COAST CRAB CAKES *with* MY FAVORITE TARTAR SAUCE

When I think about crab cakes I think about going to visit my mother's sister Martha and my uncle Gil in Maryland. They have some of *the best* crab cakes in Maryland—OMG! When I visited my aunt and uncle, we always went out for crabs, and since I wasn't too fond of cracking the shells, I always ordered crab cakes—all the meat without doing the work. And in Maryland crab cakes you get a lot of meat with very little filler—just enough to hold them together. So when I was working on my recipe for crab cakes, I wanted to make them as close as I possibly could to the ones I'd had there. Uncle Gil has passed on and Aunt Martha is now ninety-one, and whenever I go to visit her I still make sure to get some crab cakes.

If you're unfortunate enough to be allergic to shellfish or to crab, in particular, you can make these with imitation crabmeat, which is made of haddock or pollack, in the same proportions, and still get your "fix."

MAKES 6 CRAB CAKES

4 tablespoons mayonnaise
1 teaspoon minced red bell pepper
2 teaspoons minced fresh dill
1 teaspoon yellow mustard
¼ cup minced scallion
½ teaspoon chili powder
2 teaspoons Old Bay Seasoning
1 tablespoon finely chopped fresh flat-leaf parsley
1 pound crabmeat
6 tablespoons plain bread crumbs
2 eggs, beaten
½ cup panko (Japanese-style bread crumbs)
Canola oil, for frying
My Favorite Tartar Sauce (recipe follows)

1. In a bowl, whisk together the mayonnaise, red bell pepper, dill, mustard, scallion, chili powder, Old Bay Seasoning, and parsley. Place the crabmeat in a strainer and drain out all the liquid. Pick through the meat to be sure there are no stray bits of shell. Gently fold the plain bread crumbs, crabmeat, and eggs into the mayonnaise mixture, making sure the crabmeat does not break apart.

2. Divide the mixture into 6 portions of equal size and form them into patties.

3. Spread the panko on a plate and turn the crab cakes in the crumbs to coat on all sides.

4. Place them on another plate as they're done, cover with plastic wrap, and put them in the fridge for a few minutes.

5. Pour ¼ inch of canola oil into a large skillet set over medium heat. When the oil is hot, remove the crab cakes from the fridge and gently place them in the oil for 2 to 4 minutes on each side, until they are a lovely shade of brown. Take them out of the skillet and let them drain on paper towels for a few minutes before serving with the tartar sauce.

MY FAVORITE TARTAR SAUCE

2 cups mayonnaise
8 gherkins
2 tablespoons drained capers
2 tablespoons hot sauce
½ teaspoon minced fresh dill
Pinch of cayenne pepper
Salt and freshly ground black pepper to taste

1. Combine all the ingredients except the salt and pepper in a food processor and pulse until well combined. Taste, and season with salt and pepper.

2. Store any leftovers covered airtight in the refrigerator.

CANDIED BACON

This is a fun, different, and *deeelicious* snack. Crumbled candied bacon is also great sprinkled on a salad or mixed into your ground beef for hamburgers.

MAKES 3 TO 4 SERVINGS

½ pound brown sugar
1 teaspoon cayenne pepper
12 thick-cut slices of bacon

1. Preheat the oven to 375 degrees.

2. Combine the brown sugar and cayenne and spread half the mixture on a rimmed baking sheet large enough to hold the bacon in a single layer. Lay out the bacon and sprinkle it with the remaining mixture. Bake for 15 to 20 minutes. Transfer the cooked bacon to drain on paper towels and eat it hot or at room temperature.

VEGETABLE SPRING ROLLS

Traditional spring rolls may be comforting but my version is also truly American!

This is a great hors d'oeuvre to have at a party because all the components can be made in advance and the spring rolls can be assembled and fried just before serving.

You can also add a teaspoon of grated Cheddar cheese to each wrapper if you like. Mix and match the filling, using what you like and what you have on hand.

To make these truly vegetarian (and also gluten-free), once you've cooked (or reheated) the collards, rice, and yams, wrap them in a leaf of Bibb, Boston, green leaf, or another large, soft lettuce instead of the wrappers. My Vietnamese friends actually make their spring rolls in wrappers and then wrap the entire roll (wrapper and all) in a lettuce leaf. *Cam on!* That's "thank you" in Vietnamese.

MAKES 16 SPRING ROLLS

½ cup Country Collard Greens (page 172)
½ cup Rice 'n' Peas (page 158)
½ cup Mother Mary's Candied Yams (page 150)
1 tablespoon all-purpose flour
1 tablespoon water
16 spring roll wrappers
Vegetable oil, for frying
Duck sauce, for serving

1. Have the greens, rice, and yams at room temperature.

2. In a small bowl or a cup, combine the flour and water and stir to make a thin paste.

3. Working with one wrapper at a time, lay it out so that one tip is pointing away from you and one is pointing toward you. Brush the outer rim of the wrapper with the paste. Spread 1 teaspoon of the collards across the bottom, cover with 1 teaspoon of the rice, and top with 1 teaspoon of the yams.

4. Fold the bottom tip of the wrapper over the filling and roll it up tightly. Then fold in the ends so that the filling is completely encased. Repeat with all the remaining wrappers and filling. (You can also do this assembly-line style by brushing, then filling, then rolling a few at a time. I usually lay out five.)

5. Pour 2 inches of oil into a deep heavy pot and heat it to 350 degrees. Fry the spring rolls for about 6 minutes or until they are nicely browned all over. Drain on paper towels and serve with duck sauce while still hot.

ROASTED YELLOW and RED BEET SALAD

The reason to roast beets wrapped in foil is that they "bleed" a lot when cooking (and the red color really stains). In fact, according to myth, it's the red beet juice that was the original inspiration for making red velvet cake.

MAKES 4 TO 6 SERVINGS

For the beets

3 large yellow beets

3 large red beets

1½ tablespoons olive oil

½ teaspoon minced fresh thyme leaves

1¼ teaspoons kosher salt

½ teaspoon freshly ground black pepper

For the salad

4 cups baby arugula, washed and dried

½ red onion, peeled and sliced thin

¼ cup sunflower seeds

¼ teaspoon kosher salt

⅛ teaspoon freshly ground black pepper

2 tablespoons extra-virgin olive oil

1 tablespoon red wine vinegar

Shaved Parmesan cheese, for garnish

1. To make the beets: Preheat the oven to 400 degrees.

2. Cut the stems from the beets but leave a short stub at the root (to help prevent bleeding). Wash the beets and wrap them individually in foil. Set the foil-wrapped beets on a rimmed baking sheet (to catch any drips) and roast them for 50 to 60 minutes until easily pierced with the tip of a knife.

3. Remove them from the oven, open the foil (but don't remove the beets), and set them aside until cool enough to handle. Line a cutting board with paper towels (again to protect it from staining) and rub the skins off the beets with a paper towel. The skins should come off easily. If not, put the beets back in their foil and into the oven to cook a few minutes longer.

4. Cut the peeled beets into 1½-inch chunks and put them in a mixing bowl. Toss with the 1½ tablespoons of olive oil and the thyme, salt, and pepper.

5. To make the salad: In a separate bowl, combine the arugula, red onion, sunflower seeds, salt, and pepper, then drizzle with the olive oil and vinegar. Toss lightly to combine. Arrange the beets around the perimeter of a serving platter, mound the dressed greens in the center, and garnish with the shaved Parmesan.

MINI-ME BURGERS

E at two; they're small!

MAKES 8 MINI BURGERS

1 pound ground beef (I prefer 30 percent fat for this)*

2 cloves garlic, minced

1 tablespoon grill seasoning (such as McCormick Grill Mates)

3 sprigs fresh thyme, leaves chopped fine

3 sprigs fresh rosemary, leaves chopped fine

½ teaspoon red pepper flakes

1 teaspoon Worcestershire sauce

Kosher salt and freshly ground black pepper

Olive oil, for frying the burgers

8 Martin's Party Potato Rolls

. . . .

* If you like your burgers very well done, you'd be better off using
20 percent fat because it cooks faster.

1. In a bowl, combine the beef, garlic, grill seasoning, thyme, rosemary, pepper flakes, Worcestershire sauce, and salt and pepper to taste. Mix well and form into 8 mini burgers.

2. Heat 1 tablespoon of oil in a medium pan over medium-high heat.

3. Cook the burgers in the oil in batches for 4 minutes on each side or until the beef is done to your liking. Add more oil as necessary to each batch of burgers. Serve on the potato rolls.

VARIATION

Mini-Me Cheeseburgers: When the burgers are just about done, top each one with a slice of Cheddar cheese and cover the pan for about a minute to allow the cheese to melt.

Slidin' into Home

My sliders always hit a home run with guests at the restaurant. I make two kinds—one with pulled pork (see page 96) and one with short ribs (see page 107). For you at home, they're a great way to use up leftovers or to make a large quantity for parties.

Just shred and reheat the meat, add some BBQ sauce (Melba's BBQ Sauce on page 100, Sweet Baby Ray's, or your own favorite) to the beef or some cracklin' (see page 98) to the pork, and serve them on mini buns. My favorites are Martin's Party Potato Rolls.

MANDARIN CHICKEN SALAD

serve this as an appetizer on Petits Toasts garnished with a sprig of dill, but you can also have it on a bed of your favorite greens or on a roll for a fabulous lunch.

MAKES 6 SERVINGS

2 tablespoons olive oil

2 tablespoons freshly squeezed lemon juice

1 tablespoon minced fresh garlic

3 teaspoons dried oregano

½ teaspoon onion powder

1 teaspoon kosher salt

½ teaspoon freshly ground black pepper

3 skin-on boneless chicken breast halves

½ cup mayonnaise

1 ripe Hass avocado, seeded, peeled, and diced

3 fresh mandarin oranges, peeled and sectioned, or 1 (11-ounce) can of mandarin orange sections, drained

1. In a large resealable plastic bag, combine the olive oil, lemon juice, garlic, oregano, onion powder, salt, and pepper and mix well. Add the chicken breasts, massaging the mixture under the skin and into all surfaces until well coated. Close the bag and refrigerate for 1½ to 2 hours.

2. Preheat the oven to 450 degrees. Drain the marinade and transfer the chicken to a baking dish. Cover with aluminum foil and bake for 15 minutes. Remove the foil, return the chicken to the oven, and bake for another 15 to 20 minutes until the chicken is white all the way through and a meat thermometer reads 165 degrees.

3. Remove the chicken from the oven and let it cool to room temperature. Remove and discard the skin and cut the meat into bite-size pieces.

4. In a mixing bowl, combine the mayonnaise, avocado, mandarin oranges, and the chicken. Taste and add more salt and/or pepper if needed.

5. Refrigerate for 1 hour before serving.

HONEY SUCKIN' HOT WINGS

My mother and my grandmother always kept a small tin on the back of the stove where they saved their cooking oil to use again. Clearly they were onto something because that oil just kept getting better and better from all the flavorings that had gone into it! More recently, however, we've learned that there are chemical compounds in the old oil that do add flavor to the next batch of whatever you're frying, but if the oil is too old or has been used too many times, it will actually make your food taste rancid. By adding a few teaspoons of old oil to a new batch of oil you'll get the best of both worlds.

MAKES 4 TO 8 COMFORTIZER SERVINGS

For the chicken

2 pounds chicken wings

1 tablespoon granulated garlic

2 teaspoons salt

½ tablespoon freshly ground black pepper

2 cups all-purpose flour

3 cups vegetable oil

For the glaze

6 tablespoons (¾ stick) unsalted butter

½ cup honey

⅓ cup Frank's RedHot Original Cayenne Pepper Sauce or your own favorite hot sauce

To serve

½ cup grated carrots

¼ cup coarsely chopped fresh cilantro, plus a few extra sprigs for garnish

1. To make the chicken: Remove and discard the tips of the wings. Separate the drumettes from the wingettes. Place the wingettes and drumettes in a large bowl, toss with the garlic, salt, and pepper, and marinate overnight in the refrigerator.

2. When you are ready to cook the wings, make the glaze: In a small saucepan over medium heat, melt the butter and honey together. Add the hot sauce, turn up the heat, and bring to a boil. Once the mixture starts to bubble up, reduce the heat and simmer for about 5 minutes more. Remove from the heat and set aside in a warm place.

3. Remove the wings from the refrigerator and toss them with the flour, making sure they are all well coated. Let them sit in the flour for about 5 minutes while you heat the oil in a medium saucepan.

4. When the oil is hot, shake the excess flour from the wings and fry them for 15 minutes, until cooked through and golden.

5. Remove the wings from the oil with a slotted spoon and transfer them to a large mixing bowl. Sprinkle the grated carrots over the wings, add the glaze, and stir with a rubber spatula to be sure everything is well coated and the carrots stick to the wings. Scrape down the sides of the bowl to make sure you get all the yummy goodness into those wings. Sprinkle with the chopped cilantro and stir one last time. Transfer the wings to a serving platter and garnish with a few sprigs of cilantro.

COLLARD GREENS SOUP

MAKES 6 SERVINGS

8 ounces smoked turkey wings or 1 medium ham hock

4 cups chicken stock

32 ounces fresh collard greens, washed and chopped

3 potatoes, peeled and diced

1 leek, chopped

2 teaspoons Frank's RedHot Original Cayenne Pepper Sauce

2 teaspoons salt

1 teaspoon pepper

⅓ cup heavy cream

1. In a large pot, slow boil ham hocks or smoked turkey in chicken stock for about 30 minutes.

2. Add greens, potatoes, leek, hot sauce, salt, and pepper. Cover and simmer 45 to 55 minutes, until greens are tender. Make sure you check in and stir often.

3. Remove the meat and let it cool. Dice the meat and put it back into the soup mixture. Remove the soup from the heat and, using an immersion blender, slowly blend in the heavy cream. Let's do this! Gimme an "E," Gimme an "A." Gimme a "T"!

CREAMY TOMATO SOUP

Tomato soup and a grilled cheese sandwich—every American kid's definition of comfort. Now that you're a grown-up, you can make your own soup and sandwich. This soup, however, is definitely good enough to stand on its own.

MAKES 4 SERVINGS

6 tablespoons (¾ stick) unsalted butter

2 tablespoons olive oil

1 medium yellow onion, diced

3 cloves garlic, minced

½ teaspoon red pepper flakes

1 (14.5-ounce) can whole peeled plum tomatoes

1 (14.5-ounce) can fire-roasted tomatoes

3 teaspoons sugar

1 cup chicken broth

¾ cup heavy cream

½ cup sherry (optional)

6 fresh basil leaves, chopped

Kosher salt and freshly ground black pepper to taste

1. Melt the butter in a large pot over medium heat. When the butter is melted add the oil. Sauté the onion in the butter and oil until it is translucent, about 15 minutes. Stir in the garlic and red pepper flakes.

2. Slowly pour in the tomatoes with their juice and stir in the sugar. Simmer, breaking up the tomatoes with a wooden spoon, for about 20 minutes, then add the broth and continue to simmer for 20 minutes longer. Remove the soup from the heat and set aside to cool for 15 minutes. Puree with an immersion blender, or in a conventional blender, then return to low heat for 10 minutes, stirring in the cream, sherry (if using it), basil, and salt and pepper to taste.

GOLDEN SPLIT PEA SOUP

When it's cold outside, there's nothing better than a bowl of homemade golden split pea soup to warm my spirits. This recipe makes a lot of soup, but you can freeze it in one-serving portions to defrost in the microwave whenever you're in need of some warmth.

MAKES 8 TO 10 SERVINGS

2 tablespoons vegetable oil

2 cups diced Spanish onion

Kosher salt to taste

2 bay leaves

1 medium smoked ham hock (about 6 ounces)

2 cups diced celery

2 cups peeled and diced carrots

2 quarts chicken stock

1 (1-pound) bag golden split peas*

2 cups peeled and cubed white potatoes

Freshly ground black pepper to taste

. . . .

For a faster cooking time, you can soak the peas in water overnight. Just make sure you rinse them in cold water before you start the cooking process.

1. Heat the oil in a medium pot over medium heat. Add the onion, 1 tablespoon salt, the bay leaves, and the ham hock. Cook, stirring occasionally, until the onion is almost translucent.

2. Add the celery, carrots, and another tablespoon of salt. Sauté for about 5 minutes, then add the chicken stock and split peas. Bring to a boil, then turn the heat to low and simmer, stirring occasionally, for about an hour and a half or until the peas are tender.

3. Then add the potatoes and cook for about 20 minutes until tender. Remove the two bay leaves and discard.

4. Taste and season with more salt and freshly ground black pepper.

CREAM OF ASPARAGUS SOUP

MAKES 6 TO 8 SERVINGS

3 pounds of asparagus*

1 Spanish onion, chopped

½ celery stalk, chopped

2 bay leaves

2 quarts chicken stock

1½ quarts heavy cream

2 tablespoons kosher salt

1 teaspoon ground white pepper

2 quarts heavily salted water

. . . .

I prefer the thin ones because they're less woody. If you can't find thin ones, you can peel the stems with a vegetable peeler after cutting off the ends.

1. Cut off the bottom inch of the asparagus stems. Separate the tips from the rest of the stems. Set the tips aside and reserve.

2. In a pot, combine the onion, celery, bay leaves, chicken stock, and asparagus stems. Bring to a boil, reduce the heat, and simmer for 20 minutes. Add the heavy cream, salt, and pepper, and simmer for 15 minutes more. Remove the bay leaves and pour the soup into a blender or food processor. Process until smooth and strain through a fine sieve into a bowl.

3. In a small pot bring the 2 quarts of heavily salted water to a boil. Set a bowl of ice in your sink. When the water comes to a boil, add the reserved asparagus tips, and blanch for 10 seconds, then scoop them out with a slotted spoon and quickly drop them in the ice bath to stop the cooking. Taste the soup for seasoning and garnish with the blanched asparagus tips.

VEGETABLE *and* PASTA SOUP

This is my take on minestrone, so, of course, around my house we call it Melbatrone.

MAKES 8 TO 10 SERVINGS

1½ tablespoons extra-virgin olive oil

2 cups chopped Spanish onion

2 teaspoons minced garlic

1 bay leaf

1 tablespoon sea salt plus additional to taste

2 cups peeled and chopped carrots

2 cups chopped celery

½ (16-ounce) can crushed whole peeled tomatoes, drained

6 cups cold water

4 cups vegetable stock

2 cups peeled and cubed Idaho potato

½ (16-ounce) can cannellini beans, drained

½ (16-ounce) can garbanzo beans (chickpeas), drained

½ pound small pasta shells

Freshly ground black pepper to taste

1. Heat the oil in a large pot over medium heat. Add the onion, garlic, bay leaf, and ½ tablespoon of the salt, and sauté for 7 to 10 minutes, until the onion is almost translucent.

2. Add the carrots, celery, and another ½ tablespoon of salt. Sauté for about 10 minutes.

3. Add the tomatoes, cold water, and stock and bring to a slow boil.

4. After about 10 minutes, when the vegetables start to become a bit tender, add the potatoes, beans, and pasta. When the potatoes and pasta are cooked, your soup is ready.

5. Taste and reseason with more salt and some pepper if you wish.

3

MAIN CONTENTMENT: FISH, POULTRY & MEAT

COUNTRY FRIED CATFISH

We grew up eating fish, fish, and more fish. Fish is one of my favorite things to eat—especially catfish. Every Friday night when I was growing up we had catfish and grits for dinner. It's a tradition in South Carolina, so, of course, when my family moved up north, they brought that tradition with them. We also ate a lot of porgy and whiting, which, like catfish, are very inexpensive. (I actually didn't eat salmon until I was an adult.) Porgy would also be great in this recipe.

The cayenne in this recipe gives my batter a kick. If you want a pat instead of a kick, feel free to use less—or none at all. At Melba's we always serve the catfish with Chipotle Dipping Sauce. See recipe on next page.

MAKES 6 SERVINGS

1½ cups buttermilk

6 (6- to 8-ounce) catfish fillets

Canola or vegetable oil, for frying

1½ cups all-purpose flour*

2½ teaspoons Melba Spice (page 128) or seasoned salt such as Lawry's

¾ teaspoon garlic powder

1½ teaspoons freshly ground black pepper

¼ teaspoon cayenne pepper

Chopped fresh flat-leaf parsley and/or lime slices, for garnish

. . . .

When I make this catfish, I sometimes like to combine my flour with cornmeal. The proportions I use are two thirds flour to one third cornmeal.

1. Pour the buttermilk into a baking dish large enough to hold the fillets in a single layer. Add the catfish fillets, turning them to coat both sides with the buttermilk. Cover and refrigerate for at least 1 hour.

2. In a cast-iron or other deep, heavy-bottomed skillet, heat 2 inches of oil to 350 degrees.

3. Meanwhile, in a large brown paper bag or a rectangular pan, combine all the remaining ingredients except the garnish. Drain the catfish fillets and add them to the bag or pan, 2 or 3 at a time, turning them to coat evenly with the flour mixture.

4. When the oil is hot, add 2 or 3 fillets at a time and fry them for about 6 minutes, turning once after 4 minutes, until they turn pecan-brown. As the fillets are done, transfer them to a plate lined with paper towels to drain.

5. Serve hot, garnished with parsley or lime slices, along with potato salad or coleslaw and sautéed spinach or collard greens.

CHIPOTLE DIPPING SAUCE

MAKES ABOUT 1 CUP

1 cup mayonnaise
2 pieces chipotle peppers in adobo sauce (I love La Morena brand)
1 tablespoon of the adobo sauce in which the chipotle peppers are packed
2 cloves garlic
3 teaspoons freshly squeezed lime juice
1 teaspoon dill pickle relish

Combine all of the ingredients in a food processor and blend until smooth. Leftovers will keep, tightly covered, in the refrigerator for at least a month.

HONEY-GINGER PAN-SEARED BAKED SALMON

If you're talking old-time, very traditional soul food, you're probably not including salmon, simply because it can't be fried. That would be the domain of catfish (or whiting or porgy). But on our menu at Melba's, salmon is big, and for me it's become an important staple of the comfort-food repertoire. When I think of fish comfort food, I think of flounder and salmon. The latter has more flavor, it's full of healthy fish oils, it stands up well to toppings and seasonings, and it's quick and easy to cook.

Our thing is flavoring it with honey and ginger. You can substitute a tablespoon each of finely chopped dill and freshly squeezed lemon juice for the ginger and honey, but the strategy is the same: Sauté quickly in a hot pan to bring out some flavor, then add the seasonings and finish it off in the oven, which gives you time to pull together your side dishes and get it all ready to plate and serve.

For the fish, you can also substitute halibut, another meaty substantial fish that stands up well to this kind of treatment; since its fillets are a bit thicker, you may have to cook it a little longer. To check for doneness, simply flake it open from an edge with the point of a paring knife.

MAKES 2 TO 4 SERVINGS

2 tablespoons light olive oil

1 teaspoon minced garlic

4 (4-ounce) salmon fillets

1 tablespoon Old Bay Seasoning

1 teaspoon freshly ground black pepper

1 tablespoon finely chopped fresh thyme

¼ cup chicken stock (or vegetable stock)

¼ cup dry white wine

Pinch of red pepper flakes

1 tablespoon peeled and minced fresh ginger

1 tablespoon honey

4 tablespoons (½ stick) unsalted butter,
   at room temperature

½ lemon, for squeezing on the fish

1. Preheat the oven to 350 degrees.

2. Place the olive oil in a large, ovenproof sauté pan over low to medium heat. Add the garlic and sauté just until golden, then remove the garlic from the pan. Sprinkle the salmon fillets with the Old Bay, black pepper, and thyme. Place them in the pan, skin side up, and cook for 2 to 3 minutes, then turn with a spatula and cook for another 1 to 2 minutes on the other side.

3. Remove the fillets from the pan and set aside. Pour the chicken stock and white wine into the pan, raise the heat, and scrape up all the good bits stuck to the bottom. Add the red pepper flakes, the ginger, the honey, and the butter. Return the fillets to the pan and bake for 5 to 8 minutes, depending on your desired degree of doneness. Transfer to a platter, squeeze the lemon juice over all, and serve.

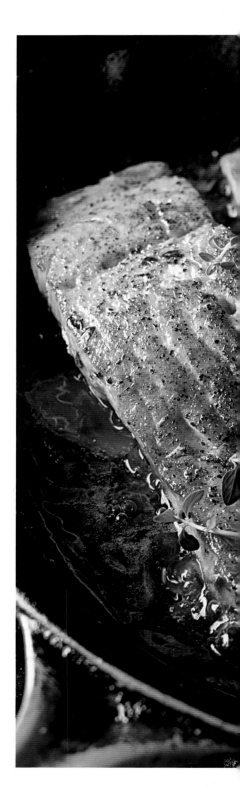

The Care and Feeding of Your Cast-Iron Pan

You may have noticed that I suggest using a cast-iron pan for many of the recipes in this book. I love my cast iron for several reasons: It gets really hot when I want it to; it creates a wonderful sear; it can go on the flame or in the oven; and, contrary to what some people might tell you, it's very easy to care for.

A friend just told me that he's still using the cast-iron skillet that was passed down to him by his mother. If cast iron were as delicate as some people seem to think, it wouldn't be so long-lived.

Yes, you do need to season it if you aren't lucky enough to have inherited one that's already been well seasoned, but it isn't that hard to do. Just put it on the stove and get it really hot, then rub it with some vegetable oil and let it cool down. Sprinkle salt to lightly cover the bottom of the pan, and rub with a clean cloth. Discard the leftover salt. Do this two or three times and your pan is seasoned. The more you use it, the more seasoned it will become—just like most things in life, practice makes perfect.

And don't believe that stuff about never washing cast iron. Soap won't hurt it and it won't destroy the seasoning. The only thing that will hurt it is sitting around in water. Remember, it's iron, and that means it rusts. So just be sure to dry it well after you wash it.

And if your mom gave you hers, don't forget to thank her.

1. Heat pan on high for 3 minutes. Remove from heat. Pour 1 tablespoon oil on 2 folded paper towels.

2. Use towels to wipe pan surface.

3. Sprinkle pan surface with 1 tablespoon coarse salt.

4. Wipe out the salt. Your pan is now seasoned!

SALMON CROQUETTES

Salmon croquettes are one of my favorite, favorite things to eat with grits. Sometimes, if we had any leftover croquettes, my mother would break them apart with a fork, add some chopped red and green bell peppers and some chopped onion, and we'd have that over rice. Waste not, want not!

MAKES 6 SERVINGS

1 (14-ounce) can pink salmon

1 large egg, lightly beaten

1 teaspoon mayonnaise

1 tablespoon diced red bell pepper

1 tablespoon diced scallion, using mostly the green part

¼ teaspoon garlic powder

½ teaspoon freshly ground black pepper

½ cup plain dried bread crumbs

1 cup vegetable oil

1. Drain the salmon, break it up, and pick out any skin or bones. Combine the salmon, egg, mayonnaise, red bell pepper, scallion, garlic powder, black pepper, and ¼ cup of the bread crumbs. Shape the mixture into 6 patties and powder them with the remaining bread crumbs.

2. Heat the oil in a medium skillet and fry the croquettes for 3 to 4 minutes on each side until golden brown.

PECAN-CRUSTED FLOUNDER

Low-fat, high-protein flounder is quickly becoming one of the most frequently consumed fish in the United States.

MAKES 4 SERVINGS

½ cup pecans

¼ cup all-purpose flour

4 (6-ounce) flounder fillets

½ teaspoon salt

¼ teaspoon lemon pepper

½ teaspoon garlic powder

4 tablespoons olive oil

1. Finely chop the pecans in a food processor and combine them with the flour in a shallow bowl. Season the fillets with salt, lemon pepper, and garlic powder, and dredge* them in the flour mixture.

2. In a large skillet, heat the olive oil over medium heat. Add the flounder and cook, in batches if necessary, 4 to 5 minutes on each side until golden.

. . . .

* When other people use this word, they want you to sprinkle flour or whatever on your food. When I say this word, I want you to really coat it . . . get it all up in there . . . don't shake off the excess!

PISTACHIO-CRUSTED GROUPER

love coating fish in nuts instead of bread crumbs to add extra flavor.

MAKES 4 SERVINGS

2 cups pistachios out of their shells
4 (6-ounce) grouper fillets
Kosher salt to taste
Freshly ground black pepper to taste
2 eggs beaten with 4 tablespoons whole milk
1 tablespoon vegetable oil

1. Preheat the oven to 300 degrees.

2. Coarsely chop the pistachios in a food processor, then spread them on a plate. Season both sides of the fillets with salt and pepper. Coat one side with the egg wash and then with the nuts, pressing gently to be sure they adhere.

3. Heat the oil in an ovenproof frying pan over medium heat. It should be hot but not smoking. Tilt the pan away from you (safety first) and gently place the fillets in the pan, pistachio side down, and cook for 4 to 5 minutes until golden brown. Flip them over and cook for another 4 to 5 minutes. Transfer the frying pan to the oven and cook for 5 to 10 more minutes, until cooked through.

FISH STEW

Yes, there are a lot of ingredients, but the pleasure of eating this healthy, hearty stew is well worth the prep!

MAKES 10 SERVINGS

2 tablespoons vegetable oil

2 cups chopped Spanish onion

2 bay leaves

2 teaspoons kosher salt

2 cups chopped celery

2 cups peeled and chopped carrots

2 cups chopped fennel

½ cup drained and rinsed capers

2 sprigs fresh thyme

½ teaspoon smoked paprika

¼ teaspoon crushed saffron threads

½ teaspoon freshly ground black pepper

4 cups white wine

1 (24-ounce) can whole peeled plum tomatoes, drained and chopped (or 10 to 12 chopped fresh tomatoes, when in season)

1 (32-ounce) bottle clam juice

2 quarts fish stock, or make your own (recipe follows)

4 cups peeled and cubed white potatoes

1½ pounds fillets of grouper, cod, halibut, or any other meaty, white-fleshed fish, cut into cubes*

½ cup chopped fresh curly parsley, for garnish

1. In a large stockpot, heat the oil. Add the onion, bay leaves, and 1 teaspoon of the salt. Sauté until the onion is almost translucent, then add the celery, carrots, fennel, capers, thyme, saffron, pepper, and the remaining teaspoon of salt. Sauté for 10 minutes, stirring frequently.

2. Pour in the wine and add the tomatoes. Bring to a boil and reduce by half, 30 to 40 minutes.

3. Add the clam juice and fish stock, bring back to a boil, turn down the heat, and simmer. Add the potatoes and cook until almost tender, 10 to 15 minutes. Remove the two bay leaves and discard.

4. Add the cubed fish and cook no more than 30 seconds. Remove the stew from the heat, ladle into bowls, and garnish each portion with chopped parsley.

HOMEMADE FISH STOCK

Head and bones of 1 (2-pound) whole grouper, snapper, cod, halibut, or any other meaty, white-fleshed fish*

2 cups peeled and chopped carrots

2 cups chopped celery

2 cups chopped Spanish onion

2 bay leaves

3 quarts water

* * * * * * * * * * * * * * *

If making your own stock, buy a whole 2-pound fish. Use the fillets for the stew and the head and bones to make the stock.

Rinse the head and bones of the fish and put them in a large pot with all the remaining ingredients. Bring to a boil, reduce the heat, and simmer for about 45 minutes. Strain, and use to make the fish stew.

CARIBBEAN SPICED SHRIMP

To quote Forrest Gump's pal, Bubba, "Shrimp is the fruit of the sea. You can barbecue it, boil it, broil it, bake it, sauté it. There's shrimp kabobs, shrimp creole, shrimp gumbo. Pan-fried, deep-fried, stir-fried. There's pineapple shrimp, lemon shrimp, coconut shrimp, pepper shrimp . . ." When I was growing up, shrimp were a big deal. Whenever they were served, we knew we had to eat as many as possible because we weren't sure when we'd have them again. And they're still my favorite go-to shellfish.

When it comes to soul food, island spices and Caribbean accents are an integral part of its roots: When our people were brought over from Africa, a lot of us were dropped off in that part of the world, where they began to add a little extra spice and a few more hits of pepper to their dishes.

I like to add some honey and pineapple juice, and even some sugar, just to mellow out the hot spice of the jerk seasoning in this dish. I would encourage you to taste whatever store-bought product you use and also to experiment if you choose to make your own marinade. In either case, you can adjust the heat to taste, adding a little more sweet or a little extra kick.

Serve the shrimp with the basmati rice on pages 113–114 or, to continue the Caribbean theme, with coconut rice. Instead of cooking your rice in either broth or water, use half water and half unsweetened, canned coconut milk.

MAKES 4 TO 6 SERVINGS

½ cup Jamaican jerk marinade (such as Walkerswood or Pickapeppa, or see recipe on next page)

4 tablespoons honey

3 tablespoons sugar, or to taste (optional)

¼ cup pineapple juice

1 pound large raw shrimp (U20), peeled and deveined*

vegetable oil for cooking

. . . .

Large shrimp are labeled U20, meaning there are up to 20 per pound. A pound of these serves four hungry diners for a main course; for an appetizer, you can buy medium shrimp and expect to serve six or more people.

1. Combine the jerk marinade, honey, sugar (if using), and pineapple juice in a nonreactive bowl and mix well. Place the shrimp in a large resealable plastic bag or other nonreactive sealable container, add the marinade mixture, and shake or stir to coat all the shrimp. Refrigerate for at least 2 hours, but preferably 24 hours.

2. To make the sauce: First, using a slotted spoon or tongs remove the shrimp from the bag or container to a plate or bowl and return to the refrigerator while you prepare the sauce. Place the strained marinade in a saucepot and bring to a boil over medium-high heat. Lower the heat and simmer for about 20 minutes or until reduced to the consistency of a warm custard sauce.

3. Preheat a grill or a grill pan. When hot, lightly brush grill with vegetable oil. Grill shrimp for about 1½ minutes per side. Don't overcook them or they will become rubbery. Serve immediately with sauce.

JAMAICAN JERK MARINADE

You can substitute one or two teaspoons of cayenne pepper and/or red pepper flakes for the Scotch Bonnet peppers. Also, you can increase or decrease the quantities of these spicy ingredients to taste. Just be careful when handling hot peppers—preferably use rubber gloves—as the juice can hurt your hands and eyes.

MAKES ABOUT ½ CUP

1 tablespoon ground allspice

4 tablespoons brown sugar

1 teaspoon ground cinnamon

1 teaspoon ground cloves

1 teaspoon ground cumin

2 or 3 cloves garlic, peeled and crushed

1 teaspoon ground ginger

1 teaspoon ground nutmeg

1 teaspoon freshly ground black pepper

1 teaspoon salt

2 Scotch Bonnet or habanero peppers, roughly chopped*

¼ cup vinegar

Juice of 1 lime

. . . .

As always, when handling hot peppers, be careful not to rub your eyes until you've thoroughly washed your hands. Using gloves is an even better idea!

Place all of the ingredients in the bowl of a food processor and pulse until well combined. The marinade is best used fresh but you can place it in a sealed nonreactive container and refrigerate for later use.

SHRIMP AND GRITS

Shrimp and grits is a traditional morning meal in the Carolina low country that may have originated with fishermen using their own catch. As far as I'm concerned, you can eat it morning, noon, or night, just so long as you eat it.

MAKES 4 SERVINGS

24 jumbo shrimp (about 15 to the pound)

For the stock

2 cups chopped Spanish onion

2 cups chopped celery

2 cups peeled and chopped carrots

2 bay leaves

1 (16-ounce) can whole peeled tomatoes, drained

1 teaspoon lobster base*

1 teaspoon Old Bay Seasoning

3 quarts water

Pinch of cayenne pepper

Kosher salt to taste

Juice of 1 lemon

For the grits

1 cup whole milk

2 cups water (plus additional at a low boil to use if necessary)

1 teaspoon kosher salt

1 cup grits (not quick-cooking)

2 teaspoons butter

¼ cup heavy cream

For the sauce

4 tablespoons (½ stick) unsalted butter

¼ cup all-purpose flour

1 tablespoon Worcestershire sauce

To cook the shrimp and serve

2 tablespoons olive oil

1 teaspoon chopped shallot

1 tablespoon minced garlic

. . . .

Lobster base is a bouillon paste in a jar. It comes in other flavors (such as chicken, beef, and vegetable) and can be found in markets where bouillon is sold, as well as online. It will keep for a long time in the refrigerator.

1. Peel and devein the shrimp. Leave the tails on, and reserve the shells. Cover and reserve prepared shrimp in the refrigerator until ready for use.

2. To make the stock: In a large pot, combine the shrimp shells, onion, celery, carrots, bay leaves, tomatoes, lobster base, Old Bay Seasoning, and the 3 quarts of water. Bring to a boil, turn the heat to low, and simmer for 1 hour. Taste and add a bit more lobster base and/or Old Bay if you think the stock needs more flavor. Transfer to a blender and blend until smooth, then line a fine sieve with cheesecloth and strain the liquid into a bowl. Measure 1 cup of stock and freeze the rest for another occasion. Put the shrimp in a bowl with the cayenne pepper and salt to taste, and drizzle with the lemon juice. Set aside.

3. To make the grits: Bring the milk, 2 cups water, and salt to a boil in a medium pot. Slowly stir the grits into the mixture, whisking constantly until well combined. Bring it back to a boil, lower the heat, cover, and simmer for 30 to 40 minutes, whisking regularly and making sure you get all the way down to the bottom of the pot so that the grits do not get stuck to the bottom. If necessary, add small amounts of boiling water to keep them from sticking. When the grits have thickened, stir in the butter and heavy cream, taste, and adjust the seasoning if necessary. Keep the grits on a very low flame and whisk periodically while you make the sauce.

4. To make the sauce: Over medium heat, melt the butter in a small saucepan and slowly stir in the flour to make a roux. Turn the heat to low and stir constantly for 7 to 10 minutes until the roux turns pecan brown. Be careful not to let it burn. Slowly stir in the reserved shrimp stock and the Worcestershire sauce.

5. To cook the shrimp: In a frying pan, heat the oil and add the shallot and garlic. Stir for 30 seconds, then add the shrimp and cook, stirring, just until they begin to turn pink. When the shrimp are almost cooked, add the sauce and simmer to thicken a bit.

6. Place grits in the center of a serving platter with the shrimp around the perimeter. Pour the sauce over the shrimp and serve.

VARIATION

Cheesy Shrimp and Grits: When the grits are done but still hot, stir in 4 tablespoons of grated sharp Cheddar cheese. That's how my son likes them.

MO'BAY SHRIMP ROLLS

This is like a lobster roll made with shrimp. Since lobster is basically from New England and shrimp are from the South—mainly around the Sea Islands of South Carolina—I decided to put my personal spin on an all-American favorite.

MAKES 6 SERVINGS

1½ pounds cooked and peeled large shrimp, cut up (about 4 cups)

4 tablespoons mayonnaise

2 tablespoons minced red onion

1 tablespoon peeled and finely chopped celery

1 tablespoon finely chopped red bell pepper

2 teaspoons finely chopped fresh tarragon leaves

2 teaspoons finely chopped fresh flat-leaf parsley leaves

2 teaspoons finely chopped fresh chives

1 tablespoon Old Bay Seasoning

½ teaspoon salt

Freshly ground black pepper to taste

½ lemon or lime

6 New England style (top-slit) or hot dog buns*

4 tablespoons (½ stick) unsalted butter, melted

1 head of butter lettuce, leaves separated, rinsed, dried, and torn into pieces

. . . .

*For hot dog buns, I prefer Martin's potato buns.

1. In a large bowl, combine the shrimp and mayonnaise, stirring gently to coat all the shrimp. Add the red onion, celery, bell pepper, tarragon, parsley, chives, Old Bay Seasoning, salt, and pepper, and stir to combine. Squeeze the lemon or lime juice over the mixture and stir again. Cover and refrigerate while you prepare the buns.

2. If using top-slit buns, open them up but leave them connected at the bottom. If the buns are not slit, slice them almost but not all the way through. Set a skillet over medium-high heat. Brush the insides of the buns with melted butter and put them buttered-side-down in the pan to brown (be careful not to burn them).

3. To serve, make a bed of lettuce in the bottom of each bun and mound the shrimp mixture on top.

BEER-POACHED BLUE CRABS

The reason I prefer male crabs is because they're bigger and meatier than females (as you might expect). One way to tell them apart is that the males actually have blue claws while the tips of the females' claws are red, as if they'd just had a manicure. There are other differences as well, but that one's my favorite.

MAKES 4 SERVINGS

6 (12-ounce) bottles pale lager beer
4 tablespoons Old Bay Seasoning
4 bay leaves
10 whole black peppercorns
1 teaspoon red pepper flakes
2 tablespoons kosher salt
12 blue crabs (preferably male)

1. In a large pot on high heat, combine all of the ingredients, except the crabs, and bring to a boil. Add the crabs, cover the pot, and cook for 10 minutes or until the crabs turn red. Remove cooked crabs to a rimmed sheet pan to cool slightly.

2. Crack the crabs with lobster crackers to get out all the good stuff!

NOT SO PO' BOYS
with TARTAR SAUCE

The po' boy is Louisiana's answer to the hero, which is also why it's traditionally served on French bread. As the name suggests, it was intended to be an inexpensive but filling meal. When made with fried oysters, however, it isn't so "po'" anymore!

MAKES 4 SANDWICHES

1 cup buttermilk
1 teaspoon Old Bay Seasoning
Salt and freshly ground black pepper to taste
1 cup all-purpose flour
2 pounds shucked oysters (I suggest Blue Points)
Vegetable oil, for frying
1 (24-inch-long) baguette cut into 4 (6-inch) lengths
2 teaspoons unsalted butter
¼ cup chopped romaine lettuce
My Favorite Tartar Sauce (page 26)
Juice of ½ lemon

1. In a bowl, combine the buttermilk, Old Bay Seasoning, and salt and pepper to taste. Place the flour in another bowl and season it with salt and pepper to taste.

2. In batches, dredge the oysters in the flour, then coat them with the buttermilk, and coat again with the flour. Set them aside as they are battered.

3. Fill a large, deep pan with vegetable oil to a depth of about 2 inches and heat it to 350 degrees. Working in batches, drop the oysters gently into the hot oil and fry for approximately 2 minutes, until they are browned and cooked through. Transfer them to paper towels to drain and, while still hot, sprinkle them with a bit of salt.

4. Cut each piece of bread in half horizontally. Melt the butter in a skillet and brown the insides of the bread.

5. Lay the bottoms of the bread on a platter (or 4 individual plates) and top each with one quarter of the romaine, one quarter of the tartar sauce, one quarter of the oysters, and a squeeze of lemon juice. Cover with the top halves of the bread and serve.

CHICKEN PERLO

Perlo has to be one of my all-time favorite dishes—the epitome of Southern comfort. Like many one-pot chicken-and-rice dishes, it's a traditional "cook up," something to make when money is short and you want a meal that's tasty and filling—a Carolina low country version of a Cajun jambalaya. It's sometimes spelled perloo and sometimes called chicken bog (according to one source because it's a "soggy, boggy mess")—although I'd never heard that term before I started looking into what might have been the origins of perlo—and it seems to be related to pilaf, pilau, and paella.

Whatever you call it, it's extremely simple and satisfying, but it has to be done right. It's all about the seasoning, baby! You'll never get a bland piece of chicken in the Deep South, and when you cook the rice in the seasoned broth from the chicken—now that's some flavor.

MAKES 6 TO 8 SERVINGS

3 pounds chicken, whole or parts (preferably breasts, thighs, and legs)

6 cups chicken broth

2 teaspoons salt

2 teaspoons freshly ground black pepper

2 teaspoons onion powder

1 teaspoon garlic powder

6 bay leaves

1 pound smoked kielbasa or sage sausage, cut in ¼-inch dice

1 large white onion, diced

1 tablespoon canola oil, as needed (max ¼ cup)

2 cups uncooked long-grain rice

1. In a 6-quart pot, combine the chicken, broth, salt, pepper, onion powder, garlic powder, and bay leaves. Bring to a boil over high heat, then reduce the heat to medium, cover, and simmer for 1 hour.

2. Take the chicken out of the broth. When cool enough to handle, remove the skin and bones, and cut the meat into bite-size pieces—or pull it apart, which is the way my grandma Amelia preferred to do it.

3. Remove the bay leaves and measure 4 cups of the broth, adding water if you don't have enough. Taste to be sure it's well seasoned. Remember, you're going to add rice, so a little extra seasoning won't hurt. If the broth isn't seasoned to your liking, now's the time to spice it up. Return the broth to the pot.

4. Put the sausage in a dry skillet and set over medium-low heat. When the sausage has rendered its fat, add the onion. If there isn't enough fat in the pan to sauté the onion, add canola oil as needed. Sauté until the onion is caramelized and the sausage is a bit brown around the edges, 5 to 8 minutes. The kielbasa is already cooked, but if you're using the sage sausage, you need to be sure that it's cooked all the way through.

5. Add the chicken, the sausage and onion mixture, and the rice to the broth in the pot. Bring to a boil, then reduce the heat to medium low, cover, and simmer for 20 minutes.

6. Remove from the heat and let the rice sit, still covered, for another 5 to 10 minutes.

7. Remove the lid and you've got it! Great country perlo, just like Grandma used to make!

RICE PILAF–STUFFED CORNISH HENS

I really love Cornish hens, and I particularly love stuffing them. There are so many different stuffings you can use—including the two variations below. It's a healthy way to eat and you get a lot of flavor from the stuffing. Put a green on the side and a salad, and you're good to go. It's a quick, tasty, fun way to cook.

MAKES 4 SERVINGS

2 tablespoons olive oil

¼ cup chopped onion

1 cup chicken stock

1 teaspoon kosher salt

3 tablespoons unsalted butter plus ⅓ cup melted unsalted butter

⅓ cup uncooked wild rice

2 (1½-pound) Cornish hens

1 teaspoon freshly ground black pepper

½ teaspoon garlic powder

½ teaspoon onion powder

1 tablespoon chopped fresh rosemary leaves

6 cloves garlic, peeled and cut in half

¼ cup water

½ cup chopped mushrooms

1. Heat 1 tablespoon of the olive oil in heavy saucepan over medium heat. Add the chopped onion and sauté for about 5 minutes until softened. Add the chicken stock, ½ teaspoon of the salt, and the 3 tablespoons of butter, and bring to a boil. Add the rice and bring back to a boil. Reduce the heat to low and simmer, covered with a tight lid (do not lift the lid), for 45 minutes. Remove from the heat and let the rice sit uncovered for about 10 minutes.

2. Preheat the oven to 400 degrees.

3. Put the hens in a medium roasting pan breast side up. Rub them with the remaining tablespoon of olive oil, and season them inside and out with the remaining ½ teaspoon of salt, the pepper, garlic powder, onion powder, rosemary, and garlic to taste. Stuff them with the wild rice pilaf and, if you haven't used all the garlic, put any remaining in the pan with the hens. Pour the water around the hens in the roasting pan.

4. Cover the roasting pan with aluminum foil and roast for 30 minutes.

5. Reduce the oven temperature to 350 degrees, remove the foil, add the mushrooms to the juices in the pan, and return to the oven for an additional 30 minutes, basting with the pan juices and the melted butter every 10 minutes.

6. The hens are done when the flesh is no longer pink, the juices run clear, and a meat thermometer inserted into the thickest part reads 165 degrees.

7. Cut the hens in half lengthwise and serve a half bird with stuffing per person.

VARIATIONS

CORN BREAD STUFFING

4 tablespoons (½ stick) unsalted butter

1 cup finely chopped yellow onion

2½ cups homemade or store-bought corn bread, cubed (or use corn muffins)

1 teaspoon chopped fresh sage leaves

1 celery stalk, diced

1 tablespoon poultry seasoning

⅓ cup chicken stock

1 tablespoon chopped fresh flat-leaf parsley leaves

1 teaspoon kosher salt

¼ teaspoon freshly ground black pepper

1. Melt the butter in a sauté pan, add the onion, and cook for 5 minutes over medium heat, until the onion is translucent. Put the corn bread cubes in a large bowl. Add the onion, sage, celery, poultry seasoning, chicken stock, parsley, salt, and pepper, and mix to combine.

2. Use to stuff the hens as directed above.

SMOKY WILD RICE STUFFING

This variation adds a little more flavor to the wild rice stuffing with sweet red bell pepper and smoky bacon fat.

> 3 tablespoons rendered bacon fat
> 2 tablespoons diced sweet onion
> 1 tablespoon minced red bell pepper
> 1 clove garlic, minced
> ⅓ cup uncooked wild rice
> 1 cup chicken stock
> ½ teaspoon kosher salt

1. Heat the bacon fat in a sauté pan over medium heat. Stir in the onion and red pepper and cook until the onion is translucent. Add the garlic and cook for just 1 minute. Add the rice and sauté for 5 minutes. Add the chicken stock and salt. Bring to a boil, reduce the heat, cover, and cook 45 minutes, until the rice is tender and easily fluffed with a fork.

2. Use to stuff the hens as directed on previous page.

SLOW-ROASTED ADOBO TURKEY

Seems like a long process, I know. But most of the time your turkey is just sitting in the refrigerator or the oven, getting better and better, while you do other things. If you're making this for Thanksgiving, or some other food-based celebration, it allows you to complete the rest of your menu without having to worry about the big bird.

MAKES AT LEAST 8 SERVINGS

1 pint distilled white vinegar

1 (14- to 16-pound) fresh turkey

¼ cup olive oil

2 large yellow onions, diced

8 cloves garlic, diced

2 teaspoons chicken base

1 teaspoon adobo seasoning

Freshly ground black pepper to taste

1 bunch of carrots, peeled and sliced in half lengthwise

1. In a large bowl, combine the vinegar with 3 pints of water and wash the turkey thoroughly, inside and out, with the mixture.

2. Heat the oil in a large skillet over medium heat and add the onions. Sauté until almost translucent and add the garlic. Sauté for another couple of minutes, then add the chicken base, adobo, and black pepper. Stir to combine the ingredients. Remove from the heat and add just enough water to make a paste—about 1 small cup.

3. Rub down the turkey, inside and out, with the paste, wrap it in plastic wrap, and refrigerate for at least 3 hours or, preferably, overnight. Remove the turkey from the refrigerator 30-45 minutes before putting in the oven to allow it to come to room temperature.

4. Preheat the oven to 400 degrees.

5. Unwrap the turkey and place it, breast side up, in a roasting pan. Brown the turkey in the preheated oven for 10 minutes, then remove the turkey and turn the oven temperature down to 200 degrees.

6. Remove the turkey from the pan and lay the carrots in the bottom in a single layer. Make sure the carrots cover the entire bottom of the pan. (The goal is for the turkey not to touch the bottom of the pan.) Add just enough water to cover the carrots, return the turkey to the pan, and cover with aluminum foil.

7. Roast in the 200-degree oven for 10 hours (I do this overnight.) Then remove and uncover the turkey, turn up the oven temperature to 350 degrees, and roast the turkey, uncovered, for 30 minutes longer.

8. Let the turkey rest for 10 to 15 minutes before carving.

Game Meats 'n' Such

My down-home country family has a long history of delicious ways to cook whatever animals they would hunt or trap in the many forests, fields, streams, and ponds around the farms where they grew up. That history and those cooking skills came down from Great-Grandmother Laura Brown to Grandma Mea, and from her to my father's and my generations.

My cousin Vern, who we call king of the wild meats, and his wife, Jeannie, always have an impressive collection of game—including fried squirrel, rabbit stew, venison, barbecued raccoon, turtle, and more—all of which Jeannie makes him keep in a separate freezer outside the house. Vern, of course, is always delighted when any of us family members inquire about his specialties. I don't know where he gets his game, and I really don't want to, but those dishes are all pretty commonplace down in our part of South Carolina. And if you want to be really authentic, you wash it all down with a jar of corn liquor (that's homemade moonshine), but don't quote me on that.

If you'd like to try cooking any of these, venison, rabbit, and even turtle meat are available from several mail-order sources. Venison and rabbit are also available at many butcher shops, especially if you order in advance. If you're looking for squirrel or raccoon, I'm afraid you're on your own.

CHICKEN *with* APPLES *and* PEARS

Easy, tasty, sweet, and savory—one of the best one-dish meals you'll ever make.

MAKES 4 SERVINGS

4 chicken drumsticks

4 chicken thighs

¼ cup garlic powder

3 tablespoons salt, or more to taste

2 tablespoons freshly ground black pepper, or more to taste

1 cup chicken stock

3 tablespoons Dijon mustard

1 tablespoon honey

4 tablespoons olive oil

4 tablespoons (½ stick) unsalted butter

¼ cup all-purpose flour

2 Granny Smith apples, peeled and sliced ¼ inch thick

1 red Anjou pear, peeled and sliced ⅓ inch thick

1 large yellow onion, peeled and sliced ¼ inch thick

4 medium Yukon Gold potatoes, cubed

1. Preheat the oven to 350 degrees.

2. Season the chicken with the garlic powder, salt, and pepper, and refrigerate for at least 3 hours to allow the flavors to meld.

3. In a small bowl, combine the chicken stock, mustard, and honey. Mix well and set aside.

4. Over medium heat, heat the olive oil in a cast-iron pan or another heavy pan that can go from the flame to the oven. Add the chicken pieces skin side down and brown for 6 minutes; turn and brown for 2 minutes on the other side.

5. Remove the chicken from the pan and add the apples, pears, potatoes, and onions. Sauté the apples, pears, potatoes, and onions until browned and remove from pan.

6. Add the butter and when the butter has melted, add the flour and stir constantly until the two are well combined. Stir in the chicken stock mixture and cook for 3 minutes.

7. Return the chicken, apples, pears, potatoes, and onions to the sauce in the pan. Bake for 25–35 minutes, until the chicken and potatoes are cooked through.

BBQ TURKEY MEAT LOAF

I use dark meat turkey for this meat loaf because it's juicier and tastier than the white meat.

MAKES 6 TO 8 SERVINGS

2½ pounds ground dark meat turkey

1 cup minced red bell pepper

1 cup minced green bell pepper

1 cup minced yellow onion

2 eggs, beaten

1 teaspoon chicken base or 1 chicken bouillon cube

1 heaping teaspoon adobo seasoning

½ teaspoon salt

¼ teaspoon freshly ground black pepper

1 cup plain bread crumbs

1 tablespoon chopped fresh mint leaves

1 cup Melba's BBQ Sauce (page 100) or my favorite bottled sauce, Sweet Baby Ray's

1. Preheat the oven to 325 degrees.

2. Put the ground turkey in a large mixing bowl and add all the ingredients except ¼ cup of the BBQ sauce. Combine thoroughly with your hands. Shape the meat into a loaf and place it on a lightly greased rimmed baking sheet.

3. Bake for 45 minutes or until a toothpick inserted in the center comes out clean. Drizzle the top of the cooked meat loaf with the remaining ¼ cup of BBQ sauce, and let it rest for at least 15 minutes before slicing.

4. Serve it with mashed potatoes and broccoli or spinach.

PULLED PORK SHOULDER

This is my dad's recipe. In North Carolina, they don't use a lot of sauce. They use mostly dry rubs and add coleslaw for wetness. But if you like, you can certainly add Melba's BBQ Sauce (page 100) or your favorite.

MAKES 8 TO 10 SERVINGS

1 (4-pound) bone-in pork shoulder

½ cup apple cider vinegar

½ cup chicken stock

1 tablespoon Worcestershire sauce

1 teaspoon molasses

1 teaspoon BBQ sauce, optional

1 teaspoon seasoned salt

1 tablespoon chili powder

¼ cup light brown sugar

¼ teaspoon smoked paprika

4 cloves garlic, peeled and sliced

1 large yellow onion, peeled and sliced

1. Pat the pork shoulder dry and score it ¼ inch apart and ⅓ inch deep in a crosshatch pattern.

2. To make the brine, line a large bowl with a large resealable plastic bag. In the bag, combine the vinegar, stock, Worcestershire sauce, molasses, and BBQ sauce (if using). Add the pork, press as much air as you can out of the bag, and seal. Refrigerate (still in the bowl) on the lowest shelf of the refrigerator for at least 12 hours.

3. When you are ready to cook the pork—or, even better, at least 6 hours before cooking—combine the salt, chili powder, brown sugar, and paprika. Remove the pork from the refrigerator and from the bag and transfer it to a large board. Pour the brine into a clean bowl, cover, and return it to the refrigerator. Pat the pork dry with paper towels. Make small slits all over the shoulder with a sharp pointed knife and insert slices of garlic into the slits. Lovingly massage the dry spice mixture into the pork.

4. At this point you can either cook the pork or, to develop even more flavor, put it into the bowl you used for brining, cover, and return it to the refrigerator for another 6 hours or overnight.

5. Let the shoulder sit at room temperature for 2 hours before cooking.

6. When ready to cook, preheat the oven to 275 degrees.

7. Spread the sliced onion in the bottom of a deep roasting pan just large enough to hold the pork. Lay the meat on top, fatty side up, and add the reserved brine. Cover the pork with parchment paper and seal the pan with aluminum foil. Cook for 6 hours or until the pork is tender.

8. When done, transfer it to a platter and strain and reserve the pan juices. Cut the skin and fat from the meat and reserve it for making cracklin' (see below). Pull out the bone or pull the meat away from the bone. Both methods work equally well. Using two forks, gently pull the meat apart into bite-size pieces.

9. To reheat, place the meat in a pan with the strained pan juices. Either preheat the oven to 250 degrees or set the pan over a low flame, cover, and heat to your desired temperature.

Cracklin' Goodness

I sometimes wonder how anything that tastes so good could be so easy to make. But it is. Cracklin' is nothing more than pork skin that's had the fat cooked out of it until it's crisp and crunchy.

Put the fat and the skin you've cut from the shoulder skin side up in a sauté pan over low heat and cook until the fat has liquefied and the skin is crisp and crackling. Remove the skin from the pan. It should form diamond shapes from having been scored before cooking. You can break it into even smaller pieces if you prefer.

Eat it on a piece of fresh rye bread or use it in your corn bread (see mine on page 156).

FINGER LICKIN' RIBS

Just about everyone has their own favorite recipe for ribs. This one is mine; and, once you've made it, it might become your favorite, too. Give yourself 24 hours for that rub to do its work. Serve the ribs with Sweet 'n' Savory Coleslaw (page 178), potato salad, and plenty of paper napkins—or just do what I do and lick your fingers.

MAKES 4 TO 6 SERVINGS

2 racks spare ribs
2 teaspoons dark brown sugar
1 teaspoon freshly ground black pepper
1 teaspoon cayenne pepper
1 teaspoon garlic powder
2 teaspoons hickory smoked salt
2 teaspoons red pepper flakes
2 teaspoons smoked paprika
Melba's BBQ Sauce (recipe follows)

1. Pat the ribs dry with paper towels. If the membrane hasn't been removed from the back part of the ribs, peel it off with a sharp knife. (It will come off easily.) Combine the sugar and all the spices to make a rub. Massage it generously all over the ribs. Place the ribs on a large sheet of heavy-duty aluminum foil and cover with a second sheet of foil. Roll up the edges of the bottom sheet all around to cover the edges of the top sheet and make sure that none of the juices can escape. Refrigerate the ribs in their foil for 24 hours.

2. Take the ribs out of the refrigerator and, still wrapped in the foil, let them come to room temperature for 30 to 45 minutes.

3. Meanwhile, preheat the oven to 300 degrees.

4. Place the ribs, still in the foil, in a single layer on a rimmed baking sheet. Reduce the oven temperature to 250 degrees and bake the ribs for 3½ hours until the meat is tender. Open the foil packages to line the rimmed baking sheet and brush the ribs with BBQ sauce. Turn up the oven temperature to 350 degrees. Return the ribs to the oven and cook uncovered for 30 minutes more. Remove from the oven and cut them apart between the bones before serving.

MELBA'S BBQ SAUCE

MAKES ABOUT 3 CUPS

> 2 tablespoons canola oil
> 2 tablespoons finely chopped onion
> 2 cloves garlic, finely chopped
> 1¼ cups ketchup
> ¼ cup molasses
> 1 tablespoon Worcestershire sauce
> ¼ cup cider vinegar
> 1¼ cups light brown sugar
> 1 teaspoon kosher salt
> 2 teaspoons smoked paprika
> 2 teaspoons chipotle powder
> 2 teaspoons dry mustard
> ¼ cup water, plus more if needed
> ¼ cup strong brewed coffee (espresso if possible), plus more if needed

1. Heat the oil in a medium saucepan over low heat. Add the onion and garlic and sauté for 5 minutes, stirring constantly. Add all of the remaining ingredients except the water and coffee. Slowly stir in the water and coffee until the mixture has the consistency of ketchup. Make sure all the sugar has dissolved. Increase the heat to medium and simmer the sauce for 20 to 30 minutes. Stir in additional water and coffee if the sauce becomes too thick.

2. Use at once or refrigerate in a tightly lidded jar. The sauce will keep for at least a month.

SMOTHERED PORK CHOPS

Serve these with mashed potatoes or rice 'n' peas and everyone at the table will be wanting to kiss the cook.

MAKES 4 SERVINGS

4 (¾-inch-thick) bone-in pork chops

½ cup buttermilk

½ cup plus 2 tablespoons olive oil

3 large yellow onions, peeled and sliced

3 cloves garlic, minced

2 teaspoons poultry seasoning

2 tablespoons minced fresh marjoram leaves

1 teaspoon paprika

Kosher salt and freshly ground black pepper to taste

1½ cups all-purpose flour

1 teaspoon cayenne pepper

2½ cups chicken broth

4 tablespoons (½ stick) unsalted butter

8 ounces sour cream

1. Put the chops and buttermilk in a large resealable plastic bag, set into a bowl, and refrigerate overnight. Remove the chops from the bag and pat them dry with paper towels.

2. Heat the ½ cup of oil in a large heavy pan, preferably cast iron, that is both flameproof and ovenproof. Add the onions and sauté for 5 to 7 minutes, until almost translucent. Add the garlic and cook for 2 minutes more. Transfer the mixture to a small bowl and set aside.

3. Season the chops with the poultry seasoning, marjoram, paprika, and salt and pepper to taste. Put the flour, cayenne, and a generous sprinkle of salt in a brown paper bag and shake to combine. Dredge the chops, one at a time, in the flour mixture.

4. Remove the chops and reserve the flour left in the bag.

5. Preheat the oven to 275 degrees.

6. Heat the remaining 2 tablespoons of oil in the same pan in which you cooked the onions and cook the chops for 5 minutes on each side or until they are browned. Remove the chops, add the chicken broth to the pan, and scrape up all the good bits from the bottom with a wooden spoon. Stir in the butter.

7. Return the chops to the pan, cover them with the reserved onions and garlic, and bake for 20 minutes, or until the chops are cooked through.

8. Meanwhile, put the sour cream in a bowl and add just enough of the seasoned flour left in the brown bag to form a paste. Slowly pour the paste into the skillet and whisk to combine the ingredients. Reduce the heat to low and cook for 5 minutes to make a gravy.

9. Now, smother those chops with the gravy and swoon!

PINEAPPLE BAKED HAM

This ham is perfect for a sit-down dinner or a party buffet table, hot from the oven or at room temp. It also makes great leftovers. But take heed: You will need to start this ham party two days in advance.

MAKES ABOUT 12 SERVINGS

For the brine

2 cups light brown sugar

6 tablespoons salt

4 cups pineapple juice

2 cups pure maple syrup

2 quarts water

For the ham

1 (6- to 8-pound) bone-in cured ham

2 tablespoons Dijon mustard

½ cup light brown sugar

Juice of 1 orange

1 teaspoon chopped fresh rosemary leaves

1 teaspoon chopped fresh thyme leaves

¼ cup pineapple juice

20 cloves

2 (12-ounce) cans sliced pineapple, drained

Small jar of maraschino cherries

1. In a pot large enough to hold the ham, combine all the brine ingredients and bring to a boil over medium-high heat. Reduce the heat and simmer for 15 minutes. Remove from the heat and allow the brine to cool to room temperature.

2. While the brine cools, rinse the ham and score the skin in a crosshatch diamond pattern, being careful not to pierce the flesh. When the brine has cooled, put the ham in the pot, cover, and refrigerate for 2 days.

3. Preheat the oven to 325 degrees.

4. Remove the ham from the brine, pat it dry with paper towels, and put it in a roasting pan. Discard the brine; it cannot be reused.

5. In a small bowl, combine the mustard, brown sugar, orange juice, rosemary, thyme, and pineapple juice. Coat the surface of the ham with the mustard mixture and stick the cloves into the top of the skin.

6. Bake for 2 hours, basting every 30 minutes with the pan drippings. Remove from the oven and decorate the surface of the ham with the pineapple rings and maraschino cherries, sticking them in place with wooden toothpicks. (Remember, plastic melts!) Return the ham to the oven and bake for 30 to 45 minutes longer, until a meat thermometer reads 150 degrees.

7. Remove when done and let the ham rest for 10 minutes before slicing and serving.

WINE-BRAISED SHORT RIBS *of* BEEF

Short ribs, to me, are the filet mignons of comfort food and great for wowing guests. This is my mom's recipe, and we would eat it on special occasions like holidays and birthdays. These ribs are stick-to-your bones good, something I think of eating when it's really cold out and I'm craving a truly hearty meal. My mom has always been big on marinating red meat. She hated the idea of biting into a nice cut of beef only to discover that—whoa— it had absolutely no taste, and she believed that marinating was the way to ensure flavor.

If you want a quick fix, this is not the recipe for you. This one is a labor of love; you have to take your time and cook it slow and long. When I cook these at home, I braise them for a good three and a half hours. I suggest you pour yourself a glass of the same red wine you use in the recipe, put on some nice music, and relax. It's all about the seduction of spices and enjoying the dream. Our criterion at Melba's is that nobody should have to use a knife; the meat should just fall off the bone. That extra hour of slow cooking really pays off.

MAKES 4 TO 6 SERVINGS

2 tablespoons minced fresh rosemary leaves,
    from 1 large or 2 medium sprigs

2 tablespoons minced fresh thyme leaves, from 3 or 4 sprigs

2 cloves garlic, peeled and chopped

1 tablespoon coarse salt

1 teaspoon freshly ground black pepper

12 to 16 short ribs of beef (about 4½ pounds)*

1 tablespoon vegetable oil, or more as needed

1 (750-ml) bottle dry red wine

4 cups beef or chicken stock

2 bay leaves

Water, as needed

. . . .

Short ribs are usually three or four to the pound, and one pound, which includes the bones, will cook down to serve only one hungry diner, with some leftovers (if you're lucky).

1. Combine the rosemary, thyme, garlic, salt, and pepper in a large resealable bag. Add the ribs, and shake the bag well to ensure that all the ribs are coated with the mixture. Refrigerate for at least several hours and preferably overnight.

2. When you're ready to cook, preheat the oven to 350 degrees.

3. Place the oil in a large, heavy, ovenproof skillet with a lid or a Dutch oven over medium heat. (It should be large enough to eventually hold all the ribs in one layer.) When the oil is hot but not smoking, brush off most, but not all, of the rub and place the ribs in the pan with at least ½ inch separating them. Brown on all sides, about 7 minutes per side. If working in batches, simply set aside the browned batch and add up to 1 tablespoon more oil to the pan if needed.

4. Once all the ribs are browned, deglaze the pan with about ¼ cup of the wine, scraping with a wooden spoon to dislodge any brown bits on the bottom. Place the ribs back in the pan in a single layer and add the rest of the wine, the beef or chicken stock, the bay leaves, and enough water (if necessary) to just cover the ribs. Raise the heat, bring the liquid to a boil, then lower to a steady simmer, cover the pan, and cook on top of the stove for about 30 minutes.

5. Transfer the entire pan, covered, to the oven and cook for 2 to 2½ hours (up to 3½ hours if you are still enjoying that "glass" of wine like me), until the meat easily falls off the bones. Remove from the oven and, using a large spoon or ladle, skim as much grease from the top of the liquid as possible. Discard the bay leaves. Transfer the ribs to a serving platter, bring the liquid in the pan to a boil over high heat, and reduce the liquid to your desired thickness to use as a sauce.

ALL-AMERICAN CLASSIC MEAT LOAF

I normally make this with beef and veal, but you can add pork, or use only ground dark meat turkey if you want to cut some of the fat. Just make sure it adds up to two pounds of meat. Covering the meat loaf while it bakes helps to keep it moist.

MAKES 8 SERVINGS

1 pound ground beef (I use 20 percent fat)

1 pound ground veal

2 teaspoons adobo seasoning

1 teaspoon garlic powder

2 eggs

1 tablespoon freshly ground black pepper

1⅓ cups Italian flavored bread crumbs

⅔ cup whole milk

2 tablespoons Worcestershire sauce

¼ cup ketchup or tomato sauce, plus additional for brushing the loaf

1½ cups finely chopped onion

½ cup finely chopped celery

⅓ cup finely chopped green bell pepper

⅓ cup finely chopped red bell pepper

1. Preheat the oven to 350 degrees.

2. Spray an 8-inch loaf pan with nonstick cooking spray.

3. Combine all the ingredients in a medium bowl and mix well with your clean hands. Transfer the meat loaf mixture to the prepared pan and pat gently to even it out. Brush the top with a bit more of the ketchup and cover the pan with aluminum foil.

4. Baked covered for 45 minutes, then uncover and bake 15 minutes longer, until the top is browned and a toothpick inserted in the center comes out clean or the temperature reaches 165 degrees on an instant-read meat thermometer.

5. Remove from the oven and allow the meat loaf to rest for at least 15 minutes before slicing and serving.

BEEF STEW OVER BASMATI RICE

Ask the butcher to cube the beef for you and you'll save a lot of time. If you're expecting a crowd, just double the recipe. A one-dish meal with no last-minute prep, this is perfect for casual entertaining.

MAKES 8 SERVINGS

For the stew

8 tablespoons vegetable oil

2 pounds London broil, cubed

2 quarts water

4 cups peeled and chopped red onion

2 cloves garlic, minced

2 bay leaves

2 tablespoons kosher salt

4 cups peeled and chopped carrots

4 cups chopped celery

2 cups red wine

2 quarts beef stock

2 tablespoons Worcestershire sauce

4 cups peeled and cubed white potatoes

2 cups cooked garbanzo beans (chickpeas)

For the rice

2 cups basmati rice

4 cups water

2 tablespoons unsalted butter

2 teaspoons salt

To serve

Chopped fresh flat-leaf parsley leaves

1. To make the stew: Heat 4 tablespoons of the oil in a large pot, and, working in batches, sear the meat until brown on all sides. Add the water, bring to a boil and reduce to a simmer until the beef starts to become tender, about 45 minutes. Strain through a sieve set over a bowl and save the liquid. Set the meat aside.

2. In a Dutch oven or heavy bottom pot over medium heat, heat the remaining 4 tablespoons of oil. Add the onion, garlic, beef cubes, bay leaves, and 1 tablespoon of the salt. Cook until the onion is almost translucent. Then add the carrots, celery, and the remaining 1 tablespoon of salt. Sauté for 5 minutes, then add the wine. Reduce the wine by half to cook off the alcohol. Add the beef stock, the Worcestershire sauce, and the reserved beef cooking liquid, and lower the heat to a slow simmer. When the vegetables are tender, add the potatoes and garbanzo beans and cook for 20 more minutes until the potatoes are tender. Remove the two bay leaves and discard.

3. To make the rice: While the stew is cooking, in a medium pot over medium heat combine the rice with the water, butter, and salt. Stir constantly until the water comes to a boil, then turn the heat to low, cover, and simmer for 12 to 15 minutes.

4. Serve the stew over the rice garnished with the chopped parsley.

KICKIN' PRIME RIB CHILI

Chili is great to serve at parties because it doesn't require last-minute fussing, guests can help themselves, and you can make it in large quantities for a crowd. I love serving my chili with sourdough or Classic Corn Bread (page 156) for dunking. Just make sure there are plenty of napkins around.

MAKES 4 TO 6 SERVINGS

2 tablespoons vegetable oil

2 pounds prime rib, cubed 1 inch*

1 Vidalia or Spanish onion, diced

2 teaspoons chopped garlic

1 jalapeño pepper, seeded and diced

2 bay leaves

1 tablespoon kosher salt plus additional to taste

2 tablespoons Worcestershire sauce

1 cup red wine

2 tablespoons tomato paste

1 (12-ounce) can whole peeled tomatoes, drained

1 quart beef stock

1 (12-ounce) can red kidney beans, drained

Freshly ground black pepper to taste

To serve

Minced scallions

Grated sharp Cheddar cheese

Sour cream

. . . .

For a less pricey chili, you can substitute chuck roast for the prime rib. It will still be delicious.

1. Heat 4 tablespoons of the oil in a large pot and, working in batches, brown the beef on all sides. Remove the browned meat and set it aside.

2. Add the remaining 2 tablespoons of oil to the pot along with the onion, garlic, jalapeño, bay leaves, and 2 tablespoons of the salt. Sauté until the onion is translucent, about 10 minutes, then return the beef to the pot along with the Worcestershire sauce and the wine. When the wine has reduced by half, add the tomato paste, the canned tomatoes, and the stock. Using two forks, break up the tomatoes.

3. Turn down the heat and simmer the chili for about 30 minutes, stirring regularly, until the beef is tender. Remove the three bay leaves and discard. Finally, add the kidney beans and salt and pepper to taste.

4. Serve with small bowls of minced scallions, grated cheese, and sour cream, and allow each diner to finish his or her chili to taste.

SAUSAGE AND RED RICE

This is a flavorful, filling, and easy one-dish meal to have with a salad on a Friday night, at the end of a busy week. Kudos to Aunt Juanita, as this recipe is her showstopper.

MAKES 4 SERVINGS

2 tablespoons olive oil

6 slices of bacon

1 yellow onion, chopped

½ yellow or orange bell pepper, chopped

½ green bell pepper, chopped

1 teaspoon minced garlic

1 teaspoon chopped fresh sage leaves

½ pound hot sausage with sage

½ pound Italian pork sausage (hot and/or sweet)

4 cups water

2 cups uncooked long-grain rice

1 (16-ounce) jar or 2 cups of your favorite homemade tomato sauce

Sea salt and freshly ground black pepper to taste

Grated Parmesan cheese

1. Preheat the oven 350 degrees.

2. Heat 1 tablespoon of the olive oil in a large pan over medium heat. Add the bacon and cook for about 10 minutes, turning to brown on both sides. Remove the cooked bacon and lay it on a paper towel to drain. Add the onion and peppers to the bacon drippings in the pan and sauté until the peppers are soft and the onion is almost translucent. Add the garlic and sage and sauté for 5 minutes more. Remove the vegetable mixture and set aside.

3. Add the remaining tablespoon of olive oil to the pan. Cut the sausage into ¼-inch-thick slices. (Some of the sausage may break up, which is fine.) Add it all to the pan and sauté for about 10 minutes until cooked through.

4. In a 2½- to 3-quart Dutch oven or an ovenproof baking dish with a lid, combine the water, rice, tomato sauce, sausage, bacon, and the vegetable mixture. Season with salt and pepper to taste. Cover the pan tightly with a lid, if it has one, or with aluminum foil and bake for about an hour or until the rice is done. Remove from the oven and set aside, still covered, for 15 minutes.

5. Remove the lid, sprinkle the rice lightly with Parmesan cheese, and serve.

GRANDMA'S FAVORITE POT ROAST

Pot roast is undoubtedly one of the top ten all-time-favorite comfort foods. On a bitter-cold snowy night, there's nothing better to warm your heart and soul. Making pot roast is a process that takes time and builds anticipation, and it's a reason for the whole family to gather in the kitchen. I'm betting that this recipe is one you and your family will turn to again and again.

MAKES 6 TO 8 SERVINGS

1 (3- to 4-pound) boneless chuck roast

Kosher salt and freshly ground black pepper to taste

1 cup all-purpose flour

6 tablespoons olive oil

1 cup chicken stock

2 cups beef stock

1 cup red wine

3 cups carrots, chopped into 1-inch lengths

2 cups chopped celery

2 cups chopped Spanish onion

6 whole cloves garlic

4 sprigs fresh rosemary

4 sprigs fresh thyme

1. Preheat the oven to 300 degrees.

2. Season the pot roast with a generous amount of salt and pepper. Coat it all over with the flour.

3. Add 3 tablespoons of the olive oil to a Dutch oven or a deep roasting pan with a lid and set it over medium heat. When the oil is hot, add the pot roast and sear it on all sides for about 8 minutes total. Remove the meat from the pan, turn up the heat, and add the chicken stock, beef stock, and red wine. Using a long-handled metal spoon or a whisk, scrape up all the good bits from the bottom of the pan.

4. Return the meat to the pan and add the carrots, celery, onion, and garlic. Tie the sprigs of rosemary and thyme together with kitchen string and add them to the pan. Cover and roast in the preheated oven for about 3½ to 4 hours, until the meat is fork-tender.

BURGUNDY-BRAISED LAMB SHANKS

Slow-cooked and falling-off-the-bone tender, these are perfect for a cold winter's night. Serve them with Yukon Gold Roasted Garlic Mashed Potatoes (page 146)—with or without the roasted garlic—to sop up the delicious braising liquid, and any green vegetable of your choice.

MAKES 4 SERVINGS

3 cups all-purpose flour

Kosher salt to taste

Freshly ground black pepper to taste

4 lamb shanks

2 to 3 tablespoons vegetable oil

4 cups chopped white onions

4 bay leaves

4 cups peeled and chopped carrots

4 cups chopped celery

2 cups Burgundy wine

1 gallon beef stock, or more as needed

2 tablespoons Worcestershire sauce

1. Season the flour with salt and pepper and spread it on a large plate. Dredge the lamb shanks in the seasoned flour.

2. Heat the oil in a deep heavy pan over high heat. Add the lamb shanks and brown on all sides for about 10 minutes.

3. Remove the shanks from the pan and lower the heat to medium. Add the onions, bay leaves, and a tablespoon of salt, and sauté until the onions are translucent. Add the carrots and celery, and sauté for about 5 more minutes. Raise the heat, add the wine, scrape up all the good bits stuck to the bottom of the pan, and cook until the wine is reduced by half, 15 to 20 minutes. Add the beef stock and Worcestershire sauce and simmer for a few minutes to allow the flavors to blend. Remove the bay leaves and discard. Taste and, if necessary, adjust the seasonings to your taste.

4. Meanwhile, preheat the oven to 300 degrees.

5. Place the shanks in a deep ovenproof pan and pour in the braising liquid. If the shanks are not completely covered with liquid, add more stock as needed. Cover the pan tightly with aluminum foil and bake for approximately 2 hours. When the meat is fork-tender, it's time to eat!

4

FRIED CHICKEN: A WORLD OF ITS OWN

MELBA SPICE FRIED CHICKEN

Some people like to keep their fried chicken simple, with nothing more than salt, pepper, and a little paprika; some put the seasoning in the flour for dusting or mix in some hot sauce with the eggs. Some people skip the egg-wash step, and put their chicken pieces, flour, and spices in a brown paper bag and shake to coat. This may be an effective shortcut, but to me, a couple extra steps are worth it. My method includes my mom's practice of marinating the meat overnight in advance so all the seasonings work their way in and you're guaranteed excellent flavor through and through. Fried chicken begs for some salt and some spice, and my favorite mix has all of that. It uses a blend of Southern favorites and adds a nice Latino accent, a nod to all the great Hispanic culture and cuisine we have in New York City.

Experienced home chefs like my mother, grandmother, and aunts know how to keep their oil hot enough instinctively, without a thermometer, eyeballing it and adjusting the heat as needed. But for anybody starting out, I highly recommend a deep-fry or candy thermometer with a clip you can attach to the side of your pot. It's important to make sure the oil is up to 350 degrees before putting the chicken in and to keep it close to that temperature throughout the frying. It should never dip below 300. Once you put the chicken in, it should maintain at a steady sizzle without popping or smoking.

If you don't have a thermometer or are brave enough to wing it, you'll know the oil is ready when you drop a little bit of flour in and it sizzles.

It's also a good idea to fry your chicken in a well-ventilated kitchen, or turn on a vent fan over your stove.

MAKES 2 TO 4 SERVINGS

1 (3½- to 4-pound) chicken, cut into at least 8 pieces

¼ cup Melba Spice (recipe follows)

About 6 cups (1 quart) vegetable oil (high-heat safflower oil is good)

4 large or 3 extra-large eggs

1 cup all-purpose flour

Salt and freshly ground black pepper to taste

1. If the breast pieces are large—and they often are with store-bought chickens these days—cut them up into smaller pieces; they can be larger than the thighs, but not twice as large. Fold the wings back over themselves so they fry as one tight unit. Place the chicken pieces in a ziplock bag or plastic container, add the spice mix and shake or spread it around so that all the chicken pieces are evenly coated. Cover the container or close the bag and refrigerate overnight.

2. When you're ready to cook, preheat the oven to about 185 degrees (no more than 200 degrees).

3. Set a rack over a baking pan or sheet pan and put it in the oven. Fill a Dutch oven or large cast-iron skillet halfway with vegetable oil and clip a deep-fry or candy thermometer on the side to gauge the temperature of the oil. Put the skillet or Dutch oven over a medium-high flame and heat to 350° F.

4. Meanwhile, beat the eggs in a large shallow bowl and place alongside a large plate containing the flour. Once the oil is hot enough, dip each piece of chicken into the egg, then dredge in the flour. Shake off any excess flour and slide the chicken pieces carefully into the oil; your best tool for this is a pair of tongs.

5. Be sure the chicken pieces are not crowded together or touching. If necessary, fry them in batches. Keep an eye on the oil temperature and adjust the heat up or down as needed; it should never be less than 300° F or more than about 380° F. If necessary, cover your cooking vessel briefly to prevent splattering.

6. Fry each piece of chicken until golden brown all over, turning it once after about 8 minutes. (This is optional if the chicken is entirely submerged in oil). Wings should take 8 to 10 minutes, drumsticks and thighs 15 to 20 minutes, larger breast pieces 20 to 25 minutes. To test, pierce with a fork or skewer close to the bone: If the juices run clear, the chicken is done. (You can also check doneness with a meat thermometer: The internal temperature should reach 140° F; this will increase to 155° F if you let the chicken rest after removing it from the oil.) As the pieces are done, place them on the draining rack in the warm oven. When all the chicken is done, taste and adjust the seasonings, and serve hot.

MELBA SPICE

You can take a shortcut and mix up several of my favorite store-bought seasonings. Or you can make your own mix from scratch, using small amounts of all the ingredients in the shortcut version. Mix ingredients in a bowl and store in an airtight jar in a cool, dark place for several months. In addition to this fried chicken recipe, I also use it in the Country Fried Catfish (page 51), and you can use it to add zest to almost any sautéed or grilled beef, lamb, pork, or chicken.

Shortcut Recipe

2 tablespoons Complete Seasoning
   (Sazón Completa or adobo seasoning)

2 tablespoons Old Bay Seasoning

4 packets Sazón Goya con Culantro Y Achiote seasoning
   (they contain 1 teaspoon each)

Homemade Melba Spice

1 tablespoon ground dried bay leaves

1 tablespoon onion powder

1 tablespoon garlic powder

1 teaspoon salt

1 teaspoon celery salt

1 teaspoon powdered (dry) mustard

1 teaspoon freshly ground black pepper

1 teaspoon smoked paprika

1 teaspoon ground celery seed

½ teaspoon ground white pepper

½ teaspoon ground nutmeg

½ teaspoon ground ginger

½ teaspoon toasted ground coriander seed

½ teaspoon toasted ground cumin seed

½ teaspoon dried oregano

¼ teaspoon red pepper flakes

⅛ teaspoon ground cloves

⅛ teaspoon ground mace

⅛ teaspoon ground cardamom

⅛ teaspoon ground allspice

⅛ teaspoon cayenne pepper (optional, for extra heat)

THROWDOWN FRIED CHICKEN

A lot of people might just give up on making fried chicken before they ever start, figuring there's no way they're going to be able to duplicate that crispy crust and moist, steamy, perfectly seasoned interior you get with a commercial deep-fryer. Might as well go to a restaurant or get takeout, right? Wrong! Great fried chicken is actually surprisingly easy to pull off at home if you just follow a few basic principles: Use a big enough pan or pot, keep the oil hot, don't crowd the pan, take your time, put a lot of love into it, and have loads of fun.

This is the chicken that, along with my eggnog waffles (see page 4), won Bobby Flay's throwdown on national TV.

MAKES 4 SERVINGS

1 (3-pound) chicken, cut into 8 pieces

2 teaspoons kosher salt

1 teaspoon freshly ground black pepper

1 teaspoon sweet Spanish paprika

1 teaspoon poultry seasoning

½ teaspoon garlic powder

1 tablespoon brown mustard

2 cups buttermilk

Peanut or vegetable oil, for frying

2 cups all-purpose flour

2 teaspoons Goya Sazonador seasoning*

. . . .

This is what I used on the Throwdown, *but you could also substitute Melba Spice (page 128) if you prefer.*

1. Put the chicken pieces in a bowl. Sprinkle with the salt, pepper, paprika, poultry seasoning, and garlic powder. Add the mustard and, using your hands (clean, of course), work all the seasonings into the meat. Pour in the buttermilk, cover with plastic wrap, and marinate in the refrigerator for at least 2 hours.

2. When ready to cook, pour 3 inches of oil into a deep, heavy-bottomed skillet (preferably cast iron) and heat to 325 degrees over medium heat.

3. While the oil is heating, combine the flour and Sazonador seasoning in a large brown paper bag. Add a few pieces of chicken at a time to the seasoned flour and shake the bag like you really mean it. Fry the chicken in batches until it is beautifully brown and crispy on one side, about 15 minutes. Then turn and cook on the other side until the chicken registers 160 degrees on an instant-read meat thermometer, about another 15 minutes.

4. As the pieces are done, transfer them to drain on paper towels.

OVEN-FRIED CHICKEN

With a lot less fat (and a lot less mess) but all the great flavor of traditional fried chicken, this is also a great way to serve fried chicken to a crowd. Just increase the quantities as needed, put it in the oven, and you're done. You can even make it in advance and serve it at room temp.

MAKES 4 TO 6 SERVINGS

6 chicken thighs
6 chicken drumsticks
1 teaspoon poultry seasoning
¼ teaspoon cayenne pepper
1 teaspoon freshly ground black pepper, plus additional to taste
¾ cup panko bread crumbs
¼ cup Italian seasoned bread crumbs
1 teaspoon salt
2 tablespoons whole milk
½ cup mayonnaise

1. Preheat the oven to 375 degrees. Spray a 9 x 13-inch baking pan with nonstick cooking spray.

2. Put the chicken in a bowl and season with the poultry seasoning, cayenne, and 1 teaspoon of black pepper. In a second bowl, combine the bread crumbs, the salt, and pepper to taste. Combine the milk and mayonnaise in a shallow dish. Dredge the chicken pieces in the milk mixture and then in the bread crumbs.

3. Lay the breaded chicken in the prepared pan and bake for 45 minutes. Then turn it over and bake for another 15 to 20 minutes until it is done. When done, it should register 165 degrees on an instant-read meat thermometer and, when pierced with a fork, the juices run clear. Transfer to paper towels to drain before serving.

MELBA'S GLUTEN-FREE FRIED CHICKEN

Many people have been discovering that they feel better when they go gluten-free, and customers often ask what we have on our menu that fits into their gluten-free diet. Since Southern fried chicken is one of our signature dishes at Melba's, I developed this recipe so that no one would ever have to feel deprived. I worked on it for more than a year to get it right, and I'm proud to say that I don't think the great fried chicken taste is compromised in any way.

MAKES 4 SERVINGS

1 (3-pound) chicken

For the marinade
1 quart milk
1 tablespoon cayenne pepper
1½ tablespoons freshly ground black pepper
2 tablespoons kosher salt
1 tablespoon onion powder
1 teaspoon garlic powder

For the flour mixture
2 tablespoons cayenne pepper
3 tablespoons freshly ground black pepper
4 tablespoons kosher salt
2 tablespoons onion powder
2 teaspoons garlic powder
2 cups brown rice flour
1 cup tapioca flour
1 cup potato starch
Vegetable oil, for deep frying
4 large eggs beaten with ½ cup water

1. Cut the chicken into 8 pieces.

2. To make the marinade: Pour the milk into a bowl large enough to hold all the chicken. Add the cayenne, black pepper, salt, onion powder, and garlic powder and whisk to combine.

3. Poke holes all over the chicken pieces with a fork and add the chicken to the bowl with the marinade. Rub the marinade into the chicken, cover, and refrigerate for 1 hour.

4. For the flour mixture: While the chicken is marinating, in a medium bowl combine all the ingredients for the flour mixture.

5. Pour the oil into a large, heavy-bottomed pan to a depth of 2½ inches and heat to 325 degrees. (You can use a deep-fry or candy thermometer to judge the temperature.)

6. When the oil is hot enough, remove the chicken from the marinade, dredge it in the egg wash, and then dredge it in the flour mixture, making sure to coat it on all sides. Cook, turning it once, until golden brown on the outside and completely cooked through, about 20 minutes. When done, it should register 165 degrees on an instant-read meat thermometer. Don't crowd the pan—cook in batches if necessary—and make sure the temperature of the oil never drops below 300 degrees. Drain the cooked chicken on a large brown paper bag, thick butcher paper, or paper towels.

Fried Chicken and Waffles: A Little Bit of History

Contrary to popular belief, chicken and waffles does not come from anywhere in the south. It comes from Harlem. The true originator of the dish—commercially speaking—was the Wells Supper Club, founded in 1938 by Joseph and Anna Wells at 132nd Street and Seventh Avenue. The Harlem Renaissance was in full swing at the time, and the club became a popular post-clubbing hangout and gathering place for hungry jazz musicians who'd finished their last set. Since there was often fried chicken left over from the dinner service, the Wellses started to offer a late-night sweet and savory combination of chicken and waffles that went down like a smooth jazz duet.

Since then, restaurants around the country have come up with their own versions of the dish. One such restaurant, Roscoe's House of Chicken and Waffles, opened in Los Angeles in the 1970s by Harlem native Herb Hudson, has attracted a devoted following of Hollywood celebs. But chicken and waffle eateries now thrive in every part of the country—from Trina's Starlite Lounge just north of Boston to Lo-Lo's in Phoenix, Maxine's in Indianapolis, and Birch & Barley in Washington, D.C.—as well as throughout the south, including Gladys Knight's in Atlanta, Bacon Bros. Public House in Greenville, South Carolina, Cowbell in New Orleans, and the Early Bird Diner in Charleston, to name just a few. Each of these claims its own special batter or seasoning, or gravy, or all of the above.

BUTTERMILK FRIED CHICKEN

Brining the chicken in buttermilk overnight produces tender, flavorful fried chicken with a thick crunchy crust. The variations below are both delicious but the crust won't be as crispy or crunchy. Try them all and see which one you like best.

MAKES 4 SERVINGS

1 (3-pound) chicken, cut into 8 pieces
2 cups buttermilk
3 cups all-purpose flour
1 teaspoon kosher salt
1 teaspoon poultry seasoning
1 tablespoon freshly ground black pepper
1 tablespoon garlic powder
1 tablespoon sweet paprika
Vegetable oil, for frying

1. Put the chicken in a large bowl and add the buttermilk, turning the chicken to be sure all the pieces are coated. Cover and refrigerate overnight.

2. Combine the flour, salt, poultry seasoning, pepper, garlic powder, and paprika in a large, sturdy paper bag.

3. Heat the oil to 350 degrees in a heavy-bottomed or cast-iron skillet. (You can sprinkle a bit of flour in the oil; if it sizzles, the oil is ready for frying.) Remove the chicken from the buttermilk and place one piece at a time in the bag with the flour mixture. Shake to coat the chicken well and place 3 or 4 pieces at a time in the hot oil. Don't overcrowd the pan or the chicken won't fry properly. Cook for 20 to 25 minutes, turning as necessary to be sure all the pieces are an even pecan-colored tan. When done, it should register 165 degrees on an instant-read meat thermometer. Remove from the oil as they're done and drain on paper towels.

4. Now I'm really getting hungry!

VARIATIONS

Fried Chicken with Hot Sauce: Skip the buttermilk and sprinkle the chicken with 1 tablespoon of Frank's RedHot Original Cayenne Pepper Sauce before dredging it in the flour mixture.

Fried Chicken with Mustard: Instead of the buttermilk, coat the chicken with 1½ tablespoons of Dijon mustard before dredging it in the flour mixture.

5

SOME JOY
ON THE SIDE

YUKON GOLD ROASTED GARLIC MASHED POTATOES

When I cook this at home I leave the skins on the potatoes. You can do what you want, but if you leave them unpeeled, be sure to wash them well!

MAKES 6 TO 8 SERVINGS

1 whole head of garlic, cut in half horizontally

1 tablespoon olive oil

2½ to 3 pounds Yukon Gold potatoes, cut into large cubes

½ cup heavy cream

4 tablespoons (½ stick) unsalted butter

½ teaspoon ground white pepper

Kosher salt to taste

1. Preheat the oven to 350 degrees.

2. Place the garlic halves on a square of aluminum foil. Moisten the skin with the olive oil, wrap them in the foil, and roast for 45 minutes, or until the garlic is tender. When it is cool enough to handle, pop the cloves out of the skin.

3. Bring a large pot of salted water to a boil. Add the potatoes and boil for 20 minutes, or until tender.

4. Drain the potatoes and return them to the pot set over low heat. Slowly stir in the cream, 3 mashed cloves of the roasted garlic,* and the butter. Now it's time to mash. Put a lot of love into the process and let go of any tension you've built up during the day.

5. When the mashed potatoes are smooth, stir in the pepper and salt to taste. Voilà! Serve right away.

. . . .

* *Put the leftover garlic in a small container with a tight-fitting lid. Cover them with extra-virgin olive oil, cover, and store in the refrigerator for future use. They will keep almost indefinitely.*

TWICE-BAKED POTATOES

These are a favorite with my teenage son!

MAKES 4 SERVINGS

4 Idaho potatoes

2 tablespoons vegetable oil

1 cup heavy cream

8 tablespoons (1 stick) unsalted butter, plus 2 teaspoons melted or clarified unsalted butter

1 cup sour cream

¼ cup shredded Cheddar cheese combined with ¼ cup shredded Gruyère cheese

3 cloves roasted garlic (see page 146)

1 teaspoon seasoned salt

Ground white pepper to taste

½ teaspoon smoked paprika, for garnish

Minced fresh chives, for garnish

1. Preheat the oven to 350 degrees. Wash and dry the potatoes. Massage the potato skins with the oil, put them on a rimmed baking sheet, and bake for 1 hour.

2. Turn up the oven temperature to 400 degrees. When they are cool enough to handle, cut the potatoes in half lengthwise and scoop out the flesh, being careful not to break the skins. Put the flesh in a mixing bowl and return the skins to the oven, skin side up, to roast for 10 to 15 minutes. Remove them from the oven and turn the heat down to 300 degrees.

3. Meanwhile, in a small saucepan bring the heavy cream to a simmer over low. Combine the warm cream with the mashed potato flesh, the 8 tablespoons of butter, the sour cream, half of the combined cheeses, the garlic, seasoned salt, and white pepper to taste. Fill the potato skins with the mashed potato mixture and top with the melted butter and the remaining cheese. Return the potatoes to the oven at 300 for about 10 minutes, or until browned to your liking. Garnish each one with a pinch of smoked paprika and a sprinkle of chopped chives.

MOTHER MARY'S CANDIED YAMS

Mother Mary was my maternal grandmother, and she *loved* candied yams. This is her recipe and my homage to her.

MAKES 6 SERVINGS

4 large yams
¾ cup orange juice
1 cup light brown sugar
2 teaspoons ground cinnamon
1 teaspoon ground nutmeg
4 tablespoons (½ stick) unsalted butter, plus more to butter the dish

1. Preheat the oven to 350 degrees.

2. Peel and slice the yams lengthwise about ½ inch thick, then cut each slice in half crosswise.

3. Combine the orange juice, sugar, cinnamon, and nutmeg in a saucepan and bring to a boil, stirring, over medium heat. Reduce the heat and cook the mixture for about 5 minutes, then add the butter and stir until all ingredients are dissolved.

4. Layer the potatoes in an 8 x 8-inch buttered baking dish, pouring some of the sauce mixture over each layer and making sure that all the slices are coated. Cover the pan with foil and bake for 30 minutes. Uncover, baste, and continue to bake uncovered for an additional 10 minutes. Try a piece to check for doneness.

Yams or Sweet Potatoes—
What's the Difference?

All my life we've called those delicious orange root vegetables yams, but, as I've learned only recently, they're really sweet potatoes. It seems that when they were first being introduced in the southern United States, producers and shippers wanted to distinguish the orange-fleshed version from the earlier white-fleshed sweet potato most Americans were used to, so they decided to call them yams, the English version of the African word *nyami*, which refers to the starchy edible root *dioscorea*. But, in actuality, sweet potatoes (*ipomoea batatas*) are an entirely different species of vegetable from yams—they're not even remotely related to one another. The U.S. Department of Agriculture, in fact, requires that the label "yam" always be accompanied by the term "sweet potato."

Well, I'm sure that's all true, but I'm still calling mine candied yams!

HUSH PUPPIES

Try these fabulous Southern staples with the Country Fried Catfish on page 51 or the East Coast Crab Cakes with My Favorite Tartar Sauce on page 26.

MAKES 8 SERVINGS

2 quarts vegetable or soybean oil

2 cups self-rising cornmeal*

2 cups self-rising flour*

¾ teaspoon baking soda

¾ teaspoon kosher salt, plus more for sprinkling

½ teaspoon sugar

1 small Vidalia onion, chopped

1 small red bell pepper, cored, seeded, and chopped

1¼ cups buttermilk

2 eggs, lightly beaten

. . . .

* Can't find self-rising flour or cornmeal? Make your own! 1 cup all purpose flour OR cornmeal, 1½ teaspoons baking powder, and ¼ teaspoon salt

1. Heat the oil in a large pot to 350 degrees on a deep-fry or candy thermometer.

2. In a large mixing bowl, combine the cornmeal, flour, baking soda, salt, and sugar. Mix in the onion and bell pepper. In a small bowl, whisk together buttermilk and eggs. Slowly pour the buttermilk mixture into the dry ingredients and mix until well combined. Gently drop the hush puppy batter into the oil 1 tablespoon at a time. Dip the spoon in a glass of cold water after each hush puppy. They're done when they turn golden brown on all sides (you may need to flip them in the oil) and rise to the top, about 6 minutes. Drain them on paper towels and sprinkle with salt.

VARIATION

Hush Puppies with Jalapeño and Creamed Corn: Leave out the red bell pepper and add 1 jalapeño pepper, seeded and diced, and 1 (8.25-ounce) can of creamed corn to the batter. Cook as described above.

BUTTERMILK BISCUITS

Give me biscuits any time of day—with bacon and eggs in the morning, with chicken and white gravy for dinner, with fried chicken (instead of waffles), all alone with syrup or molasses, or just out of the oven with gobs of melting sweet butter.

MAKES ABOUT 12 BISCUITS

2 cups self-rising flour (White Lily is my favorite!), plus more for dusting

¼ teaspoon baking soda

1 teaspoon kosher salt

5 tablespoons cold unsalted butter plus 1 tablespoon melted unsalted butter

¼ cup cream cheese, at room temperature

1 cup buttermilk, or more as needed

1. Preheat the oven to 450 degrees.

2. Line a baking sheet with parchment paper. In a large bowl, combine the flour, baking soda, and salt. Using an electric mixer or a food processor with a pastry blade set on pulse, add little pieces of the cold butter, one by one, and bits of the cream cheese until the dough forms pea-size bits of butter/cream cheese.

3. Using a rubber spatula, fold in the buttermilk. Make sure to incorporate all of the flour from the sides of the bowl. Add more buttermilk if necessary, to keep the dough soft, but be careful not to overwork it or it will become tough. Lightly flour a work surface and dust your hands with flour. Turn the dough out onto the floured surface and gently pat it out into a 1-inch-high circle or rectangle.

4. Use a 2-inch-round cookie cutter to cut out the biscuits. You can press the extra pieces of dough together to make a few more biscuits. Transfer the biscuits to the prepared baking sheet with a metal spatula, placing them close together but not touching. Brush the tops of the biscuits with the melted butter and bake for 15 to 20 minutes.

DEEP-FRIED POLENTA CAKES

Many people are confused about the difference between grits and polenta. Some people think it's all in the name and depends upon whether you're Italian or from the American South. Some think it's that polenta is made from yellow corn and grits from white corn. They're both made from stone-ground cornmeal, but according to Glenn Roberts, founder of Anson Mills in South Carolina, they're made from two very different types of corn, and because of that, grits tend to be looser and polenta a bit chewier. Others think that difference lies in the milling process itself. I'm not going to be the one to solve that riddle, but whatever you call yours, try this recipe. You won't be sorry.

MAKES 8 TO 10 (3-INCH-ROUND) CAKES

2 cups heavy cream

1 cup water

Pinch of cayenne pepper

1 bay leaf

Kosher salt to taste

1 cup polenta (not instant)

6 tablespoons grated Parmesan cheese

3 tablespoons olive oil, or more as needed

1. In a saucepan, combine the heavy cream, water, cayenne, bay leaf, and salt. Bring to a boil and taste the liquid. It needs to have enough salt for the seasoning to stand up to the heavy cornmeal without getting lost. Slowly whisk the polenta into the boiling liquid. Once it is all incorporated, switch to a wooden spoon and stir frequently until the polenta is thick. Add 4 tablespoons of the Parmesan cheese and immediately turn off the heat.

2. Line a small baking dish or rimmed baking sheet with parchment paper or plastic wrap and pour in the polenta. Put it in the refrigerator to cool. Once it has cooled, cut it into circles with a 3-inch-round cookie cutter.

3. Heat 2 tablespoons of the olive oil in a pan and fry the polenta cakes for about 3 minutes on each side until golden brown. If you are doing this in batches, you may need to add more oil to the pan. As the polenta cakes are done, transfer them to a serving platter and sprinkle them with the remaining 2 tablespoons of Parmesan.

CLASSIC CORN BREAD

Corn bread is great for dunking in your chili. When I'm eating a nice bowl of chili on a cold winter's night, I love to snuggle up in a blanket, hold that bowl in both hands, and stare at the corn bread as it slowly soaks into the chili.

If you happen to have made pulled pork, or any other recipe that provides cracklin' (see page 98), give yourself a special treat and put some in your corn bread batter.

MAKES 12 TO 14 SERVINGS

2 cups all-purpose flour

1⅓ cups yellow cornmeal, plus extra for dusting the pan

4¼ teaspoons baking powder

1 teaspoon salt

3 eggs

1⅔ cups buttermilk

⅔ cup melted unsalted butter, plus butter for greasing the pan

½ cup sugar

1. Preheat the oven to 450 degrees.

2. In a bowl, combine the flour, cornmeal, baking powder, and salt. In another bowl, combine the eggs, buttermilk, melted butter, and sugar. Stir the egg mixture into the flour mixture.

3. Grease a 9-inch cast-iron skillet or a 9 x 13-inch baking pan with butter and dust it with a little cornmeal. Pour the batter into the pan and bake for 30 minutes, until the top is golden brown and a toothpick inserted in the center comes out clean. Let the cornbread cool a bit before slicing and serving.

RICE 'N' PEAS/PEAS 'N' RICE

Mr. B., one of our cooks at the restaurant, is from Jamaica, and he calls this dish rice 'n' peas, which threw me at first because I grew up calling it peas 'n' rice—and to make things even more confusing, the "peas" are actually beans!

MAKES 6 SERVINGS

½ cup dried red kidney beans

1 small onion, diced

2 cloves garlic, minced

3 sprigs fresh thyme

1 bay leaf

1 (14-ounce) can coconut milk

1 teaspoon salt

1 teaspoon freshly ground black pepper

2 teaspoons adobo seasoning

6 cups water

4 cups uncooked white rice

4 tablespoons (½ stick) unsalted butter

1. Combine all the ingredients except the rice and butter in a large pot with a tight-fitting lid and cook uncovered over medium-low heat for 1½ hours.

2. Add the rice and butter, bring to a boil, reduce the heat, cover, and simmer for 30 minutes, or until the liquid has been absorbed and the rice is fluffy.

3. Remove from the heat and let sit for 10 minutes. Remove the bay leaf and thyme sprigs, and serve.

MELBA'S TRES MAC & CHEESE

(See page 163 for photo)

Of course macaroni and cheese is a staple of modern soul food, but I consider it one of the ultimate crossover dishes, an all-American favorite, loved and cherished in all neighborhoods, all cuisines, all countries, all over the world. Grown-ups love it, grandmas and grandpas love it, and, most important, kids crave it. We all scream for mac and cheese! And these days, it seems like there's an infinite number of fun variations. It's an all-purpose dish that works equally well as a side or a main course. You can use different types of pasta, different blends of cheese—it's fun to experiment— and add anything from bacon to green peas, turkey to broccoli.

MAKES 4 TO 6 SERVINGS

8 ounces elbow macaroni

For the cheese sauce

2 cups heavy cream

8 ounces sharp Cheddar cheese, shredded (about 1 cup)

6 ounces pepper Jack cheese, shredded (about ⅔ cup)

1 tablespoon onion powder

1 tablespoon garlic powder

1 tablespoon salt, or more to taste

1 teaspoon freshly ground black pepper, or more to taste

1 large egg, lightly beaten

6 ounces mozzarella cheese, shredded (about ⅔ cup)

1. Cook the macaroni in boiling, salted water until al dente. Drain, and shock in cold running water to stop the cooking. Set aside.

2. Preheat the oven to 350 degrees.

3. Place the cream in a medium saucepan over low heat and bring to a simmer, stirring frequently. Stir in half the Cheddar and half the pepper Jack along with the onion powder, garlic powder, salt, and pepper. Temper the egg by adding a small amount of the hot cheese sauce and stirring gently. Continue adding small amounts of sauce until the egg is very warm but not cooked like scrambled eggs. Just before removing the sauce from the flame, stir in the egg followed by two thirds of the mozzarella. Adjust the seasonings to taste.

4. Place the macaroni in a 9x13 baking dish, or one large enough to mix ingredients safely. Pour in the cheese sauce, then add the remaining pepper Jack and mozzarella and half the remaining Cheddar. Mix well and distribute evenly. Sprinkle the last of the Cheddar on top, cover the pan with aluminum foil, and bake for 30 minutes. Just before it's done, remove the foil to allow the top to brown.

5. Serve hot or let it cool gradually to room temperature, then cover with plastic wrap and refrigerate. Before reheating, bring back to room temperature and stir in additional shredded cheeses and cream to moisten. Bake in a preheated 350-degree oven until hot.

The Verdict Is In

When I was deciding what to serve at my restaurant, I narrowed the mac and cheese options down to four. Then I had four of my son's friends over to test them. Kids are the best testers. There's no shame in their game: They keep it real and honest and they don't worry about hurting anybody's feelings. They'll let you know straight up what's yucky and what's yummy. Imagine four little Marcus Samuelssons and Alton Browns—when they were about five years old—sitting in our apartment kitchen, seriously savoring my candidates. It was a unanimous decision, and the recipe that appears here is still the one we make every day.

SUNDAY BEST MAC & CHEESE

On Sundays my family goes from house to house visiting cousins. It's a family day when we all want to look and cook our best. This is my "Sunday best" mac and cheese.

MAKES 6 TO 8 SERVINGS

½ pound (2 sticks) unsalted butter

½ cup all-purpose flour

1 cup whole milk

3 cups heavy cream

Kosher salt to taste

Freshly cracked black pepper to taste

1 pound elbow macaroni

2 cups plus 2 tablespoons shredded extra-sharp Cheddar cheese

2 cups shredded smoked Gouda cheese

2 cups shredded Gruyère cheese

2 cups shredded Asiago cheese

1 cup grated Parmesan cheese

1 cup plain bread crumbs

1 tablespoon minced fresh flat-leaf parsley leaves

1 tablespoon snipped fresh dill

1 tablespoon finely chopped fresh oregano leaves

1. Preheat the oven to 350 degrees.

2. Bring a pot of heavily salted water to a boil and cook the pasta until it is al dente. While the pasta is cooking, melt the butter in a large saucepan over low heat and slowly whisk in the flour. Cook for about 5 minutes until well combined. Whisk in the milk and heavy cream.

3. Remove the pan from the heat as soon as the cream starts to thicken and season with salt and pepper. Return the pan to medium heat and whisk in 2 cups of the Cheddar, the Gouda, Gruyère, and Asiago. Drain and pour the pasta into the sauce, mixing until it is completely coated.

4. Combine the bread crumbs and herbs in a small bowl.

5. Transfer the pasta to an ovenproof crock or baking dish and top it with the remaining 2 tablespoons of Cheddar, the Parmesan, and the herbed bread crumbs. Bake uncovered for 20 to 30 minutes until the top is browned and the macaroni and cheese is bubbling.

Melba's Tres Mac & Cheese (see page 160)

FRIED GREEN TOMATOES

Green tomatoes are just tomatoes than haven't ripened, so I tend to serve this in the summer when local tomatoes are growing. The tomatoes are great with anything cooked on the grill for a summer treat, but I also love them with pulled pork, pork chops, or any grilled or sautéed chicken. Just don't pair them with anything else that is breaded.

MAKES 4 SERVINGS

> 4 large green tomatoes
> 4 large egg whites
> ½ cup buttermilk
> ½ cup self-rising flour
> ½ cup panko bread crumbs
> ½ cup yellow cornmeal
> 1 teaspoon seasoned salt
> ½ teaspoon freshly ground black pepper
> Peanut oil, for frying

1. Slice the tomatoes into ⅛-inch-thick rounds.

2. In a medium bowl, whisk the egg whites and buttermilk together.

3. Combine the flour, bread crumbs, cornmeal, seasoned salt, and pepper on a dinner plate.

4. Dip the tomatoes in the egg and buttermilk mixture, then dredge them in the flour mixture, making sure they are coated on all sides. You can pat the slices gently to make sure the breading adheres. Just be careful not to bruise the tomatoes.

5. Pour the peanut oil ½ inch deep into a skillet. When it is nice and hot, carefully add the tomatoes and fry over medium heat for 5 minutes. Then turn them over and fry for about 3 more minutes on the other side. When done, drain on paper towels.

LOW-COUNTRY OKRA

As a kid, I grew up saying "Okra, no! It's slimy, totally unattractive, and it doesn't look like anything anyone would want to eat, especially me." It wasn't until my mom cut it, seasoned it, fried it, and *made* me try it that I said, "Wow, this is something I want in my life for-eeeever! How did I ever live without it?" And so began the love affair between me and okra—not Oprah . . . okra! (Love her too, though.)

Once okra is fried, it's not slimy. I like mine crunchy on the outside and nice and juicy on the inside.

MAKES 6 TO 8 SERVINGS

2 pounds fresh okra, washed and drained

1 cup all-purpose flour

½ cup stone-ground cornmeal

¼ teaspoon cayenne pepper

¼ teaspoon garlic powder

1 teaspoon salt

½ cup buttermilk

4 cups vegetable oil

Salt and freshly ground black pepper to taste

1. Cut the okra into ½-inch-thick rounds. Combine the flour, cornmeal, cayenne, garlic powder, and salt in a bowl.

2. Line a plate or a baking sheet with paper towels.

3. Put the buttermilk in a separate bowl. Pour the oil into a Dutch oven or heavy frying pan, making sure that it comes no more than halfway up the sides of the pan, and heat it on medium high to 350 degrees. You can use a deep-fry or candy thermometer to test the temperature, or just sprinkle some flour in the oil. If it sizzles, the pan is hot enough.

4. Working in batches, dip-dab the okra in the buttermilk and then in the flour mixture. Shake off any excess flour and gently place the okra in the oil. Let it cook until it browns on all sides, 3 to 4 minutes altogether. Remove it from the oil and set it on the paper towels to drain. While still hot, season the okra with salt and pepper to taste.

5. Ready to eat? Serve it as a side dish instead of collards, kale, or spinach. Sometimes I mix it with corn kernels or with tomatoes and onion. Can you say "Yum"?

CORN AND OKRA SUCCOTASH

Succotash is traditionally made with corn and lima beans, or sometimes with other types of shell beans. This is my own riff on that traditional American favorite.

MAKES 4 SERVINGS

2 tablespoons olive oil

½ cup chopped Vidalia onion

1 jalapeño pepper, seeded and finely chopped

2 cloves garlic, minced

3 cups fresh corn kernels (about 4 medium ears of corn)*

1 cup fresh okra sliced into ¼-inch-thick rounds

1 cup diced fresh tomato

2 teaspoons cider vinegar

¼ cup chopped fresh basil leaves

Sea salt and freshly ground black pepper
  to taste

. . . .

To remove the kernels, shuck the corn, stand the cob on end, and run a sharp knife between the cob and the kernels from top to bottom on 4 sides.

1. Over medium-high heat, heat the olive oil in a pan large enough to hold all the vegetables.

2. Add the onion, jalapeño, and garlic, and sauté for 5 minutes, or until the onion is tender.

3. Add the corn, okra, and tomato. Cook, stirring constantly, for about 15 minutes.

4. Stir in the vinegar and basil and season with salt and pepper to taste.

BRUSSELS SPROUTS *with* APPLEWOOD-SMOKED SLAB BACON

know that some people claim to "hate" Brussels sprouts, but I think this recipe just might be the one to convert those haters to lovers. And if not, it just means there's more for me!

MAKES 4 TO 6 SERVINGS

¼ pound applewood-smoked slab bacon
1½ pounds Brussels sprouts
Kosher salt to taste
1 tablespoon honey
Freshly ground black pepper to taste

1. Cut the bacon into ¼-inch-wide strips. Heat a frying pan over medium heat, then add the bacon and cook, stirring constantly, until it is crisp—even a bit overcooked. Remove from the heat and pour out half the drippings.

2. Wash the Brussels sprouts, remove the outer leaves, and cut the sprouts in half. Bring a pot of heavily salted water to a boil over high heat, add the sprouts, cover, and cook for 10 to 15 minutes until the stem ends are tender when pierced with a sharp knife. Return the pan with the bacon and drippings to medium heat. Drain the Brussels sprouts and add them to the frying pan. Season with the honey, salt, and pepper to taste. When heated through, they're ready to eat.

COUNTRY COLLARD GREENS

Collards are bitter greens traditionally grown in the South and considered food fit for the slaves. They are a cruciferous vegetable (along with broccoli and others), and we now know that they are packed with nutrients, including vitamin C, folate, manganese, and calcium, among others, and are probably one of the healthiest vegetables around. (Kale, move on over!) My grandmother traditionally cooked them with a ham hock, and you should feel free to replace the smoked turkey wings in this recipe with a ham hock if you prefer. The brown sugar in this recipe also counteracts the bitterness of the greens, and I like mine with the little bit of spice provided by the hot sauce. They won't taste hot—just very flavorful.

MAKES 4 TO 6 SERVINGS

3 cups chicken stock

1 cup water

2 pounds fresh collard greens

½ pound smoked turkey wings

2 yellow onions, chopped

4 cloves garlic, minced

½ teaspoon light brown sugar

2 tablespoons sea salt

1 tablespoon freshly ground black pepper

1 teaspoon red pepper flakes

2 tablespoons unsalted butter

1 tablespoon apple cider vinegar

1 tablespoon hot sauce of your choice

1. Bring the chicken stock and water to a boil in a large, heavy pot over medium heat.

2. Wash the greens thoroughly in cold running water and cut off the tough stem ends. Lay the greens on top of one another and cut them into ½-inch-wide slices.

3. Put them in the boiling water along with all the remaining ingredients. Stir, reduce the heat to low, and cover.

4. Cook on low for 45 to 60 minutes, stirring every 15 minutes, until the greens are tender.

VARIATION

Vegetarian Collards: To make this dish vegetarian simply substitute vegetable stock for the chicken stock and leave out the turkey wings. They won't taste exactly the same, but they will definitely be tasty.

Potlikker

No, it won't get you drunk. Potlikker (or pot liquor) is the word, probably originating in the South, that refers to the liquid left in the pot after something—in this case collards—has been cooked, usually with some pork (such as my grandmother's ham hock). It's very flavorful and very healthy to sip on, or use it for dunking your corn bread.

SAUTÉED KALE and MUSHROOMS

There are so many great prewashed greens available these days that there's just no excuse for not eating kale or any other healthy dark green leafy vegetable.

MAKES 3 TO 4 SERVINGS

2 tablespoons unsalted butter

1 pound shiitake mushrooms, cleaned and sliced

Kosher salt to taste

2 tablespoons olive oil

½ teaspoon sliced garlic

½ Spanish onion, diced

1 head of kale, washed and chopped (or 1 bag prewashed)

Pinch of ground nutmeg

Freshly cracked black pepper to taste

1. Melt the butter in a medium saucepan. Add the mushrooms and a pinch of salt, and sauté until all liquid from the mushrooms has evaporated and the mushrooms are tender. Remove from the pan and set aside.

2. Wipe the pan clean, add the olive oil, and wait about 20 seconds for the oil to get hot. Add the garlic and onion and stir for 30 seconds.

3. Add the kale, mushrooms, a pinch of nutmeg, and salt and pepper to taste, and sauté for about 2 minutes, just until the kale is wilted. Taste, adjust the seasoning if necessary, and serve.

STEAMED BROCCOLI *and* GARLIC

This is a much more flavorful way to steam broccoli than in the traditional vegetable steamer.

MAKES 4 SERVINGS

1 bunch of broccoli

4 cloves garlic

¼ cup extra-virgin olive oil

2 tablespoons chicken stock

½ teaspoon kosher salt

2 teaspoons freshly squeezed lemon juice

1 teaspoon freshly grated lemon zest

1. Cut the stem end off the broccoli and cut the head into florets.

2. Lay the florets flat in a wide saucepan with a lid. Add the garlic, olive oil, chicken stock, and salt.

3. Set the pan, partially covered, on medium heat. After 5 minutes you should see steam. Lower the heat as much as possible and steam for another 10 minutes, until the broccoli is fork-tender and bright green.

4. Transfer to a serving bowl, sprinkle with the lemon juice, toss with the zest, and serve.

SWEET 'N' SAVORY COLESLAW

Sometimes I make this with half green and half red cabbage so that the colors really pop!

MAKES 6 CUPS

¾ cup mayonnaise, or to taste

2 tablespoons sweet pickle relish

¼ teaspoon salt

¼ cup sugar

3 cups peeled and shredded carrots

1 (3-pound) head of green cabbage, shredded

¼ cup thinly sliced scallions, green part only

¼ teaspoon celery seed

1. In a medium bowl, whisk together the mayonnaise, relish, salt, and sugar.

2. Add all of the remaining ingredients and mix to combine well.

3. Refrigerate for at least 4 hours and mix again just before serving.

Mayo-less Coleslaw

Some people prefer their coleslaw with little or even no mayo. Maybe that's how your mama made yours. It's more a German-style dish, almost like a pickled relish, and that's good, too. I just happen to like mine with lots of mayo, the way my own mother made it.

6
SWEET SURRENDER

GRANDMA MEA'S SWEET POTATO PIE

"My oh my, sweet potato pie!" There's nothing better. I'm pretty sure that as soon as the doctor told my mother it was okay for me to have solid food, she started feeding me some of that pie puree. No doubt this explains my love of this food: When I hear some is coming, I think, "Yum, goody," and my eyes start to get bigger. It's also why I sign all my notes and letters "Hugs and sweet potato pie," and if it's a really special friend, "Hugs and sweet potato pie kisses."

Sweet potato pie is as sacred to us Southerners as apple pie is to the entire nation. It's an iconic dish, the Holy Grail of our cuisine, right up there with fried chicken. If you can't make a great one, don't claim to be a real Southern cook. And please don't ever mistake it for pumpkin pie. There may be a physical resemblance but that's where it ends.

This recipe, along with many others, was passed down from my grandmother. It's as simple, foolproof, and delicious as they come—and there is no better comfort-food dessert. Sweet potatoes hold a special place in African-American culture because they reminded our ancestors who were brought over from West Africa of the yams that were a staple of their native cuisine.

You can eat the pie warm or at room temperature, plain or with whipped cream or vanilla ice cream. I fully confess to having had it for breakfast with my coffee on more than one occasion. To be honest with you, I'm looking for any excuse to eat some.

1½ pounds sweet potatoes, peeled and cut into large chunks

8 tablespoons (1 stick) unsalted butter, cut into 8 pieces

¼ teaspoon pure vanilla extract

½ teaspoon ground nutmeg

½ teaspoon ground cinnamon*

2 large eggs, well beaten

⅓ cup sweetened condensed milk

1 cup sugar**

1 (10-inch) pie crust (recipe follows, or substitute frozen)

. . . .

I like to add cinnamon to my pie filling, although a lot of the recipes I've come across—including Sylvia's and those of some of the ladies from Hemingway, South Carolina—skip it.

**Feel free to alter the amount of sugar, depending on how much (or how little) of a sweet tooth you have.*

1. Preheat the oven to 350 degrees.

2. Cook the sweet potatoes in a large pot of boiling water for 20 to 30 minutes, until tender. Remove from the heat and drain the potatoes, reserving 3 tablespoons of the cooking water. Then return them to the pot with the reserved cooking water. Stir in the butter, mashing the potatoes with a fork or a handheld blender, until well combined. Stir in the vanilla, nutmeg, cinnamon, eggs, and condensed milk. Finally, stir in the sugar and continue stirring vigorously until all ingredients are combined into a smooth pie filling.

3. Spoon the filling into the pie crust and smooth the top. Bake for 45 minutes, or until the filling is firm and a toothpick inserted into the center comes out clean.

4. Let the pie cool a bit before you try to cut it.

PIE CRUST

MAKES 1 (10-INCH) PIE CRUST

1½ cups all-purpose flour, plus more for dusting

1 tablespoon sugar

½ teaspoon salt

4 tablespoons (½ stick) cold unsalted butter, cut into pieces

½ cup vegetable shortening, chilled

3 tablespoons ice water, plus more as needed

1. Combine the flour, sugar, and salt in a large mixing bowl. Cut in the butter with a pastry cutter or two small knives until loosely incorporated into the flour mixture. Add the vegetable shortening and cut some more, until you have a loose, chunky dough with pieces of shortening the size of small peas. (Alternatively, place the flour mixture in the bowl of a food processor, add the butter, and pulse about 5 times. Then add the vegetable shortening and pulse another 5 times, until the dough forms.)

2. Lightly flour a clean work surface. Add the water to the dough and toss to moisten, pressing the dough lightly with your hands or a rubber spatula. Add an extra tablespoon of water if the dough doesn't readily moisten or come together. Place the dough on the work surface and form it into a ball, then press it into a disk about 4 inches in diameter. Wrap the dough in wax paper or paper towels and refrigerate for at least 1 hour or up to overnight.

3. Place a large sheet of wax paper on a clean work surface and sprinkle with flour. Place the dough on the wax paper and roll it out to a circle 12 to 13 inches in diameter and ⅛ inch thick. Place a 10-inch pie plate centered upside down on the dough circle and carefully turn the paper and pie plate over so the dough is in the plate. Fold the overlap underneath the edges to form a thicker rim. Refrigerate for ½ hour.

4. Preheat the oven to 350 degrees.

5. Remove the pie pan from the fridge and cover the empty, uncooked crust with aluminum foil, leaving an overhang. Fill it with uncooked beans to keep it from rising, and bake for 10 minutes. Remove the beans and foil, and prick the surface of the crust with a fork at 1-inch intervals. Return it to the oven and bake for another 10 minutes, until golden brown. Allow it to cool before proceeding with the pie recipe.

Gifts from Grandma Mea

I knew my aunt Dona was in possession of some of my grandmother's original handwritten recipes—the ones she taught me by example when I was little—so when I started writing this book I asked Aunt Dona to send them up to me. A few days later, I opened the envelope postmarked Hemingway, South Carolina, and held them in my hand.

I didn't cry at my grandmother's funeral, because she had prepared me so well for her passing. She prayed out loud twice a day, every day, so I knew her prayers by heart. And she always mentioned something like, "Lord, once I've done all that you put me here to do, please prepare me a home in the heavens . . ." But when I opened that envelope and saw my grandmother's handwriting, with her beloved recipes on scraps of paper and the backs of envelopes, I sat down at my kitchen table and cried.

PEACH MELBA COBBLER

I f you hate making pie crust, this is the recipe for you. It has all the elements of a delicious peach pie and a crust you don't have to roll out.

MAKES 8 SERVINGS

For the filling

10 fresh, ripe peaches

1 cup light brown sugar

1 teaspoon ground cinnamon

½ teaspoon ground nutmeg

2 teaspoons cornstarch

2 teaspoons freshly squeezed lemon juice

¼ teaspoon freshly grated lemon zest

½ teaspoon pure vanilla extract

For the topping

2 cups self-rising flour

1 cup granulated sugar

2 teaspoons baking powder

½ teaspoon baking soda

½ teaspoon salt

¼ teaspoon ground cinnamon

¾ cup melted unsalted butter

1 cup whole milk, at room temperature

½ teaspoon cinnamon sugar

1. Preheat the oven to 350 degrees.

2. To make the filling: Peel the peaches, cut them in half lengthwise, and remove the pit, then slice the flesh into 3 to 4 wedges (as you would if you were making lemon wedges). In a large bowl, combine the peaches, brown sugar, cinnamon, nutmeg, cornstarch, lemon juice, lemon zest, and vanilla. Transfer the peach mixture to a 2-quart baking dish and set aside.

3. To make the topping: In another bowl, combine the flour, sugar, baking powder, baking soda, salt, and cinnamon. Then blend in the melted butter and slowly stir in the milk.

4. Pour the batter over the peaches and sprinkle with the cinnamon sugar.

5. Bake for 30 to 35 minutes, until the peaches are tender and the crust is golden brown.

6. Serve the cobbler hot or at room temperature, by itself or with vanilla ice cream or crème fraîche. You probably won't have any leftovers, but if you do, store them, covered, in the refrigerator.

HONEY BUN CAKE

f you love sticky buns (and who doesn't), you'll definitely love this cake. If you love it as much as I do, it might not make twelve servings after all.

MAKES ABOUT 12 SERVINGS

For the batter

4 large eggs, at room temperature, lightly beaten

8 ounces sour cream, at room temperature

⅔ cup melted unsalted butter

½ cup water

2¼ cups cake flour*

For the filling

1 cup chopped pecans

1 cup light brown sugar

1 teaspoon ground cinnamon

¼ teaspoon ground nutmeg

For the glaze

1½ cups confectioners' sugar

1 teaspoon pure vanilla extract

4 tablespoons whole milk

• • • • • • • • • • • • • • • •

To make your own cake flour: Carefully measure out the amount of all-purpose flour required in the recipe (2¼ cups). Remove and discard (or return to the bag) 4½ tablespoons (2 tablespoons for each cup). Put the remaining flour in a sieve set over a bowl and add 2½ tablespoons of cornstarch. Sift the flour and cornstarch together 5 times. Voilà—your own homemade cake flour!

1. Preheat the oven to 350 degrees.

2. To make the batter: In a large bowl, combine, eggs, sour cream, butter, and water, then fold in the cake flour. To make the filling: In a small bowl, combine the pecans, brown sugar, cinnamon, and nutmeg.

3. Spray a 9 x 13-inch baking pan with nonstick cooking spray. Pour half of the batter into the pan and top it with the filling. Gently spread the filling with a knife to cover the batter. Top the filling with the remaining half of the batter. Bake for 40 minutes or until a toothpick inserted in the center comes out clean.

4. Just before the cake is done, make the glaze: In a small bowl, combine the confectioners' sugar, vanilla, and milk. Remove the cake from the oven and pour the glaze over the top, fully covering the cake. Let the cake cool a bit to let the glaze solidify. Serve warm or at room temperature.

UNCLE HERMAN'S SOUR CREAM POUND CAKE

My friend Michael gave me this recipe from his uncle Herman many years ago. I know it isn't the historical method of using equal parts butter, sugar, eggs, and flour (originally one pound of each) with no leavening at all, but the sour cream makes this version especially moist, and it really is a great cake. So thank you, Uncle Herman, wherever you are!

MAKES 8 TO 12 SERVINGS

3 cups all-purpose flour

1 tablespoon salt

1 tablespoon baking soda

½ pound (2 sticks) unsalted butter (save the wrappers), at room temperature

3 cups sugar

5 large eggs, separated

1 pint sour cream

1 tablespoon pure vanilla extract

1. Preheat the oven to 300 degrees.

2. In a large bowl, combine the flour, salt, and baking soda and mix well.

3. In a second bowl, with an electric mixer, beat the butter and sugar together on high for 5 minutes, stopping once or twice to scrape down the bowl.

4. Still beating, add the yolks to the butter and sugar mixture one at a time. Continue beating while you gradually add the sour cream. Next, beat in the vanilla extract. Finally, beat the flour mixture into the butter mixture. Be sure to scrape down the sides of the bowl again to incorporate all of the ingredients.

5. In a separate bowl, beat the egg whites until fluffy, then fold them into the batter.

6. Grease a 10-inch Bundt pan with the butter remaining on the insides of the butter wrappers you saved. Spoon the batter evenly into the pan and bake for 1 hour and 15 minutes to 1 hour and 30 minutes, until the top is golden and a toothpick inserted in the center comes out clean.

7. Cool the cake in the pan, then hit the side of the pan a couple of times with a fork (or knock it against the counter) and shimmy it from side to side before covering it with a plate and turning the cake out.

UNCLE ROY'S APPLESAUCE SPICE CAKE

This is it—my baking debut—except that when I made it for Uncle Roy, I left out the brown sugar. He thought it was pretty sweet anyway. Now I make it with brown sugar for my family.

MAKES 3 SERVINGS: YOU, ME, AND UNCLE ROY (OTHERWISE MAKES FOUR 4-INCH SQUARES)

8 tablespoons (1 stick) unsalted butter, at room temperature, plus more for greasing the pan

1 cup light brown sugar

1 teaspoon pure vanilla extract

1 large egg, beaten, at room temperature

2 cups chunky applesauce

2 cups all-purpose flour, plus more for dusting

1 teaspoon baking soda

1 teaspoon ground cinnamon

¼ teaspoon ground nutmeg

¼ teaspoon ground allspice

1. Preheat the oven to 350 degrees.

2. In a large bowl, cream together the butter, brown sugar, and vanilla. Add the beaten egg and the applesauce and mix well. In a medium bowl, combine the flour, baking soda, cinnamon, nutmeg, and allspice. Make a well in the center of the flour mixture, add the butter mixture, and stir until well combined.

3. Lightly grease and flour an 8-inch-square baking pan. Pour in the batter and bake on the middle shelf of the preheated oven (don't slam the door!) for 25 to 35 minutes, or until a toothpick inserted in the center comes out clean and the top springs back when pressed lightly.

4. Let the cake rest for 20 minutes before serving.

APPLE FRITTERS

Serve these with a scoop of vanilla ice cream for a fabulous fall dessert.

MAKES ABOUT 20 FRITTERS

4 cups vegetable oil

1½ cups all-purpose flour

2 teaspoons baking powder

1 teaspoon sugar

½ teaspoon salt

1 tablespoon ground cinnamon

¼ teaspoon ground nutmeg

⅓ cup whole milk

2 eggs, beaten

⅓ cup apple cider

Dash of pure vanilla extract

1 tablespoon applesauce

2 cups peeled and grated sweet apples, such as Gala or McIntosh

½ cup confectioners' sugar

1. Heat the oil in a deep fryer to 350 degrees.

2. In a large mixing bowl, combine the flour, baking powder, sugar, salt, cinnamon, and nutmeg. Stir in the milk, eggs, cider, vanilla, and applesauce. Add the grated apples and combine thoroughly. The batter will be thick and sticky.

3. Using two teaspoons, take a spoonful of batter in one hand, and push it off the spoon into the oil with the second spoon. The fritters will puff up as they fry. Work in batches and make sure the fritters don't stick together. Fry for about 7 minutes or until golden brown. Carefully remove them from the oil with a slotted spoon and drain on paper towels. Dust with confectioners' sugar and serve warm.

MOLTEN CHOCOLATE PEANUT BUTTER PETITE CAKES

Better than the best peanut butter cups you could ever imagine.

MAKES 12 CAKES

14 ounces semisweet chocolate, broken up

7 tablespoons unsalted butter, plus additional for greasing the muffin cups

1 cup granulated sugar, plus additional for the muffin cups

4 eggs plus 4 egg yolks

½ cup all-purpose flour

1 level cup plus 2 level teaspoons cold creamy peanut butter

Confectioners' sugar, for serving

Vanilla ice cream (optional)

1. Preheat the oven to 400 degrees. Butter 12 muffin cups and sprinkle them with granulated sugar.

2. In a double boiler over low heat, stirring constantly, melt the chocolate and the butter together. Make sure the water in the lower pot does not touch the bottom of the top pot or the chocolate will scorch.

3. In a large bowl, whisk together the eggs, egg yolks, flour, and granulated sugar. When the egg mixture is well combined, whisk in the slightly cooled melted chocolate mixture. Fill each prepared muffin cup halfway with the chocolate mixture, spoon 1½ level tablespoons of peanut butter into the center of each cup, and top with more chocolate mixture. Do not overfill the cups.

4. Bake for 14 minutes or until the top center crust bounces back when you press it gently.

5. Carefully pop the cakes out of the cups, garnish with a sprinkling of confectioners' sugar, and serve warm, with a scoop of vanilla ice cream if you wish.

'NILLA BANANA PUDDING

Think of this as the quintessentially Southern version of a classic icebox cake, with banana pudding instead of the whipped cream, vanilla wafers replacing the chocolate ones, and a frothy meringue to top the whole thing off. If you were in my house, this wouldn't serve eight to ten!

MAKES 8 TO 10 SERVINGS

For the pudding and layers

3 cups whole milk

¾ cup sugar

⅛ cup cornstarch

4 egg yolks, at room temperature

2 teaspoons pure vanilla extract

1 tablespoon unsalted butter, at room temperature

1 box vanilla wafers

5 very ripe bananas, sliced thin

For the meringue

3 egg whites

4 teaspoons sugar

1 teaspoon pure vanilla extract

1. To make the pudding and layers: In a medium saucepan over low heat, whisk the milk, sugar, and cornstarch together until the sugar dissolves, about 3 minutes. Slowly add the egg yolks, whisking constantly so that the eggs don't scramble. Bring to a low boil, whisking constantly, and cook until the pudding thickens, 6 to 8 minutes. Remove the pan from the heat, stir in the vanilla and butter, and set the pudding aside to cool.

2. Meanwhile, preheat the oven to 350 degrees.

3. Cover the bottom and sides of a 9 x 13-inch baking dish with a single layer of vanilla wafers. Cover the wafers on the bottom with a layer of cooled pudding, then add a layer of sliced banana. Repeat the layering process with the remaining pudding and bananas.

4. To make the meringue: In a large bowl, beat the egg whites with an electric mixer until they form soft peaks, then slowly beat in the sugar and increase the speed of the mixer until the whites form stiff peaks. Add the vanilla and beat just until incorporated, 15 seconds.

5. Spread the meringue over the top of the pudding and bake for 10 to 15 minutes. Let the pudding cool before serving.

7

A LITTLE LIQUID COMFORT

BLUEBERRY LEMONADE

To spike the lemonade, add two ounces of plain or blueberry-flavored vodka to the mixture before serving.

MAKES 12 TO 14 SERVINGS

5 cups cold water
1 cup sugar
2¼ cups fresh blueberries
1½ cups freshly squeezed lemon juice
Ice cubes
1 lemon, sliced thin, for garnish

1. To make a simple syrup, heat 2 cups of the water and the sugar in a saucepan over high heat, stirring until the sugar dissolves. Remove from the heat and set aside.

2. In a blender, combine 2 cups of the blueberries and 1 cup of the water, and puree. In a half-gallon pitcher combine the remaining 2 cups of water and the lemon juice with the blueberry puree and enough of the simple syrup to achieve your desired sweetness.

3. Serve in 8-ounce glasses over ice, garnished with the remaining blueberries and the lemon slices.

SWEET MINT ICED TEA

n the South, sweet tea can be *really sweet*! If you prefer yours less sweet, add less of the simple syrup.

MAKES EIGHT 12-OUNCE SERVINGS

8½ cups water
6 Lipton tea bags
½ cup sugar
1 cup fresh mint leaves
Ice cubes

In a pot, bring 8 cups of the water to a boil with the tea bags. Once the water has boiled, remove the pot from the heat and let the tea steep until it reaches the strength you desire. Remove the tea bags. In a small saucepan, combine the remaining ½ cup of water with the sugar and the mint leaves and bring to a boil, stirring until the sugar is dissolved. Remove the simple syrup from the heat and set aside to cool. Strain out the mint leaves, and add enough syrup to achieve your desired sweetness. Stir to combine. Serve in 12-ounce ice-filled glasses.

CUCUMBER SPLASH

MAKES 1 DRINK

1 thick and 1 thin slice of peeled cucumber

1½ ounces Hendrick's gin*

1 ounce St-Germain elderflower liqueur

½ ounce freshly squeezed lemon juice

Ice cubes

Splash of club soda

. . . .

Hendrick's gin is infused with rose and cucumber, which is why I use it in the Cucumber Splash.

Muddle the thick cucumber slice in the bottom of a cocktail shaker. Add the gin, St-Germain, and lemon juice. Add ice and shake. Double strain the drink into an ice-filled rocks glass and add a splash of club soda. Stir gently, and garnish with the thin cucumber slice.

HARLEM NIGHT

The muddled blackberries give this drink the color of a Harlem night sky.

MAKES 1 DRINK

4 blackberries

1½ ounces Courvoisier Exclusif cognac

¾ ounce freshly squeezed lemon juice

¼ ounce agave syrup

Ice cubes

Champagne float

Muddle the blackberries in a cocktail shaker. Add the Courvoisier, lemon juice, and agave. Add ice, shake, and double strain into a Champagne coupe. Float the Champagne on top.

MUY FRUITY SANGRIA

I like to marinate the orange slices, lemon slices, and blueberries in the rum before using them to garnish the sangria.

MAKES TWO 16-OUNCE DRINKS

3 ounces apricot brandy

2 ounces peach nectar (I like Looza brand)

2 ounces mango nectar (Looza again for me)

1 ounce spiced rum (such as Myers's or Captain Morgan)*

16 ounces red wine (preferably merlot)

Ice cubes

Orange slices, for garnish

Lemon slices, for garnish

Fresh blueberries, for garnish

. . . .

If you don't have spiced rum, just use any dark rum.

Combine the brandy, juices, and rum in a large pitcher. Stir in the wine and refrigerate for at least 2 hours. Fill two 16-ounce glasses with ice, pour the sangria over the ice, and garnish with the fruit.

PEACH MELBA JULEP

Two things Harlem has in common with the Kentucky Derby are juleps and fabulous hats.

MAKES 1 DRINK

6 fresh mint leaves, plus 1 mint sprig for garnish

¾ ounce brown sugar simple syrup*

3 ounces peach puree

2 ounces Jefferson's bourbon (or your own favorite)

Ice cubes

. . . .

* To make brown sugar simple syrup, combine equal parts brown sugar and water in a small pan and stir over heat until the sugar dissolves. Cool before using.

Muddle the mint leaves with the simple syrup in a cocktail shaker. Add the peach puree and the bourbon. Shake, and pour into an ice-filled rocks glass. Garnish with the mint sprig.

THE BELTON

In case you were wondering, this is named after a good friend of mine, who introduced me to it.

MAKES 1 DRINK

Ice cubes
1 ounce vodka
2 ounces coconut rum (I prefer Malibu)
3 ounces pineapple juice
Dash of grenadine
Orange slice, for garnish

Fill a highball glass with ice. Combine the vodka, rum, and pineapple juice in a martini shaker and shake for about 20 seconds. Strain the mixture into the ice-filled glass, add a splash of grenadine, and garnish with the orange slice.

HEMINGWAY

I don't know who named this a Hemingway or why, so don't ask. I know there are other drinks named for Ernest Hemingway, but they're made with rum and citrus. The classic Hemingway daiquiri is made with the juice of two limes, a grapefruit, two ounces of rum, and a quarter ounce of Luxardo or maraschino cherry liqueur. This one is actually a twist on the cocktail James Bond ordered in *Casino Royale*, but his didn't include any bitters, and his lemon peel wasn't flamed.

MAKES 1 DRINK

1 ounce vodka (Tito's or your own favorite)
1 ounce gin (Plymouth or your own favorite)
1 ounce Lillet Blanc
Dash of orange bitters
Twist of lemon peel, flamed, for garnish
Ice cubes

Combine all of the ingredients except the lemon peel in a cocktail shaker. Add ice, shake, and double strain into a Champagne coupe. Garnish with the flamed lemon peel.

ACKNOWLEDGMENTS

Atria Books/Simon & Schuster!!!!!! Can I say, ATRIA BOOKS!!!! Future authors, I am here to tell you that BIG dreams really do come true!! If I can, you can, too!

Leslie Meredith, thank you for believing in me, taking a chance on me, and having so much patience with me.

My Atria family, Sara DeLozier, xoxxo and xoxoo there is no better team!!

Laura Dail, my literary agent and my friend, you saw the light and read the words even before I could write them. I am grateful for your vision and for guiding me on this journey.

Judy Kern, Tutti Frutti? One day you MUST tell me what that means!! Two pens, one voice! I truly respect and adore your gifts, your talent—simply YOU! I could never thank you enough!

Laurie Knopp, Studio 129 Laurie, like it or not you have a friend in me until the end. Thank you for making sure the food was the star of this book!

Melissa Hom, you break the rules of photography and deliver exquisitely beautiful pictures! Can I eat the book??

Kysha Harris, my dear friend, recipe tester, culinary producer, and great chef. Team IShop stands strong!

Yvette Hayward, thank you for believing in me from infinity and beyond! You remain my ride or die sista!

Dwayne Ashley, my brother, my friend. Straight no chaser, your continuous support means the world to me.

Sabrina Lamb, six books and counting? I salute and love you 4 ever my sista-friend!

Lu Willard and Stan Hoffman—Salif and I love you both for all that you are and all that you do.

Andrew Maloney.

Toby Shorter, my attorney and friend, you are the engine that steers the train!

Michael Belton, everything NUMBERS and I love you for it!

NYC Hospitality Alliance, One Stop Shopping! Thank you for guidance and leadership in this food and beverage world that consumes me!

Shawn Thorne, you are an amazing chef and I appreciate you!

Drew Nieporent, you continue to be a wonderful friend, a true teacher, and a great mentor. Thank you for seeing the glitter of a diamond in me, way back when.

Bobby Flay, *Throwdown with Bobby Flay* really did change my life and remains a top feather in my cap. Thank you for the opportunities!

Marcus Samuelsson, always selfless, one who cares so deeply about so many. You are blessed—your kind spirit and warm heart remain intact since the very first time we met in 1993. Thank you for caring and for sharing, my friend.

My mom, thank you for life lessons, love, and for allowing me to burn and to cook. Thank you for feeding my heart and my soul.

My dad, my father, thank you for teaching me how to roast pork, pour my heart into cooking, take chances, win or lose, brush myself off, and get back in the race.

Jonathan Wilson, you are still my favorite brother. Okay, my only brother, but still my favorite.

Adrella Wilson, life is like clay to mold, shape, and make out of it whatever you'd like. I have a lot of faith in you! You always were the smartest of us three . . . xoxo!

Nicole Wilson, my only niece, live, love, and write. Perhaps you should write to live and to love.

To all my cousins, aunts, and uncles, thank you for all your support and for eating my cooking during the experimental stages! :) There is no stronger love than the love I have for all of you.

Aunt Dona Davis, my love for you overflows like the River Jordan. Besides, you know where all the spatulas are buried!

My son, Salif—because of You . . . I CAN, because of You . . . I STAND, because of You . . . I AM!

To my staff, friends, and guests at Melba's 114 and Melba's Catering, I salute you and sincerely appreciate your continued support, for without it NONE of this would be possible.

To all of you who always wanted to write, are reading this, and will try because I did, I say, "If I can, so can you!"

INDEX

ABOUT THE AUTHOR

MELBA WILSON is the owner of a growing culinary empire based in New York's famed Harlem neighborhood, Melba's 125, Melba's Catering, and her renowned restaurant, Melba's, a hot spot for celebrities, locals, and tourists from around the world who crave unbeatable American comfort food. She began her career at Sylvia's Restaurant, where she launched the popular Sunday Gospel Brunch, and has received numerous accolades and awards for her entrepreneurship and her original and family recipes. She won on an episode of the Food Network's *Throwdown with Bobby Flay,* was featured on *The View,* and appears regularly on television, most recently on CNBC's reality show *Consumed.* She lives in New York with her son, Salif.